THERE GOES
THE NEIGHBORHOOD

THERE GOES THE NEIGHBORHOOD

Protecting Your Home and Community from Poor Development Choices

Kim Patrick Kobza

NEIGHBORHOOD AMERICA PRESS

Published by Neighborhood America Press
Naples, Florida

Editing: Constance Packer Buchanan, Crosswicks, New Jersey, and Fred Kameny Columbia, South Carolina

Design and Layout: Carleton J.Giles, Group 1 Graphic Design & Exhibits Columbia, South Carolina

Illustration: Walter Fournier, Naples, Florida

Dedication

To the unsung heroes of neighborhood and community associations who take the time to care about and shape the future of their communities. To the many citizens who lead the charge in organizations dedicated to protecting the natural habitats and resources that make America special. To the many professionals who care about their communities and who work for responsible development. To my family and many friends for their patience and support, foremost, my father James J. Kobza and mother Clara Ann Kobza, both people of extraordinary intellectual courage and integrity, and my brothers and sisters Chantel, Craig, Vicki, Paul, Jeanne, David, and Beth.

Finally, I would especially like to dedicate this book to the memory of my uncle, and good friend to many, the Honorable Michael Eugene Kobza. Mike was a well known Circuit Court Judge in Muskegon, Michigan who never tired of providing leadership to his community—a truly special person.

Contents

Preface

This book is about change, not how to fight it but how to direct it. It is about growth, not how to stop it but how to shape it. Most of all it is about development choices and how we make them, as neighborhoods, as communities, and as a country. The goal here is to help communities make choices that withstand the test of time by approaching them with intellectual honesty and an understanding of process.

It is my hope that our collective intellect will overcome our greed, that we will understand that growth can be qualitative, not merely quantitative, measured not only in cubic yards of concrete but also in the valuable experiences that planning and vision can provide. Perhaps, as a society, we will accept the importance of living in harmony with our environment rather than leaving this revelation to future generations. Our challenge is to create communities and neighborhoods reflecting balance in our relationship to the land, and to each other.

Many of us wonder: How many oil slicks must wash upon the shores of America's beaches, how many of America's rivers do we have to pollute, how many of America's farmlands do we have to lose to suburbs, concrete expressways, and walled subdivisions, before we wake up to the fact that there must be limits to the destruction of our natural environment? Couldn't we attack the challenge of community planning as fervently as we send astronauts into space, build weapons of destruction, and spend to construct palatial stadiums for the games people play?

Parcel by parcel, block by block, neighborhood by neighborhood, community by community, we are losing our quality of life, all for want of attention, because we don't have the time to devote ourselves to making sure that our living environment is balanced and our development decisions rational. By training our intellect on the choices we make, we can make better choices.

As a land use attorney, I am often amazed at the lack of depth and clarity in crucial decisions about how land is to be developed. And yet in virtually every state, county, city, and town in this country such decisions, often preceded by bitter community dialogue, are made with surprising regularity.

For many communities, citizen apathy is not the primary obstacle to making informed development choices. The primary obstacle is a misunderstanding of process. Citizens, like knights of old, fight battles with pluck but not strategy. They also lack the technical resources to promote effective public debate.

This book is designed to provide you with insight into the process of challenging development that threatens your home, business, or community. It is not a book of formulas. It does not pave a single path to success. The suggestions here may not work in every situation. Every community's needs and choices are unique. But if you absorb the thoughts expressed here, and adapt them to your environment, chances are that any debate over a particular use of the land around you will be more productive and strategic. And the better the debate, the better will be the ultimate decisions affecting your quality of life.

There Goes the Neighborhood is intended to provide you, as a citizen seeking direction, with strategic ideas for confronting undesirable change in your community. The advice offered here is presented in the hope and belief that your involvement will make a difference.

I would like to express my gratitude to a number of people who were instrumental in reviewing and helping to guide this work. Specifically, my thanks go to Dr. Faye Biles, former chancellor at Kent State University; Andrea Clark Brown, chairman of the planning advisory board for the City of Naples, Florida; Ms. Susan Delegal, former Broward County attorney and current partner with the Florida law firm of Holland and Knight; Mr. Michael Davis, member and chairman of the Collier County (Florida) Planning Commission; Mr. Phil DePasquale, member of the City of Naples community services advisory board; Mr. Art Jacob, community leader and president of Neighborhood Associations of North Collier

County; Mr. Paul Muenzer, past chairman of the Regional Planning Council of Southwest Florida and ex-mayor of the City of Naples, Florida; Ms. Dollie Roberts, president of d/b/r marketing; and Ms. Terri Tragesser, past president of the Pine Ridge Property Owners Association and community leader in North Naples, Florida.

I would especially like to recognize and thank Mr. Richard Armalavage, MAI, a noted appraiser and feasibility expert. I would also like to thank Constance Buchanan, who served as my primary editor and who added invaluable insight to this work, and Randall Stevens and Archvision, of Lexington, Kentucky, who helped me with illustrations and shared insights on animation and visualization technologies.

My gratitude is also extended to the attorneys and staff of my law firm, Treiser, Kobza, and Volpe chartered, of Naples, Florida, for their support. Similarly, my many thanks to Burt and Emily Marks for their direction and guidance.

I would also like to thank my finish editor, Fred Kameny, and design and layout artist, Carleton J. Giles, together with artist Walter Fournier, who collectively contributed an extra special effort evident in their work.

Finally, my sincere thanks to Catherine Fry, Director of the University of South Carolina Press, who provided invaluable guidance to bring this work to fruition.

THERE GOES
THE NEIGHBORHOOD

Part 1

THE NEIGHBORHOOD CHALLENGE

CHAPTER I

Your Neighborhood

*B**am!!* Your life just changed. How did you first hear about the development proposal? This morning's paper? A telephone call from your neighbor? A neighborhood meeting? Or did the bulldozers just appear on your doorstep?

Much of what you value—your security, the look of your community, peace and quiet—is about to change. And why? Because a neighbor, developer, or government agency is developing the land with limited consideration for how it might affect adjacent uses, perhaps your home or business. Development is often justified in lofty economic terms and with the conviction that unbounded discretion to develop one's property is constitutionally guaranteed.

In northwest Arkansas, a local company proposes a landfill on Hobbs Mountain despite a state prohibition against siting landfills within two miles of major watersheds. The two-mile radius, which includes homes with 157 wells, 144 year-round springs, and 70 seasonal springs, lies within an area that opponents of the landfill view as geologically unstable (*Northwest Arkansas Times,* April 28, 1996).

In Idaho, the governor signs an agreement with the federal government that would allow for the storage of nuclear waste in the southeastern part of the state for a period of forty years (*Wood River Journal,* February 14, 1996). In Pennsylvania, a waste disposal firm searches for a municipality willing to serve as a harbor for the storage of low-level radioactive waste (*Wilkes-Barre Citizen's Voice,* April 30, 1996).

Residents throughout the country wonder why politicians support the expenditure of millions of dollars for professional stadiums that often threaten the fabric of neighborhoods in which they are built. While those communities build monuments to the games people play, the City of Albuquerque, New Mexico hopes to cut through part of the Petroglyph National Monument to make way for a new expressway, an action opposed by native Pueblo Indians who consider the Monument sacred (*New York Times,* January 25, 1998). Similarly, the residents of the village of Los Ranchos, New Mexico fight the construction of a bridge across the Rio Grande through their peaceful valley community (*Silicon Mesa News,* May 1996).

In Marco Island, Florida a group of local residents proposes filling a tidal lagoon and adjacent barrier island that serves as a Critical Wildlife Area for migratory birds. The residents view the lagoon as a safety hazard that impedes their path to the beach. The barrier island is one of the few remaining nesting areas in the southeastern United States for approximately twenty species of birds traveling from the Northeast to South America and back again.

In the Research Triangle of North Carolina, farmers wonder how to protect their land and way of life from rapidly encroaching urban development (*Raleigh News & Observer,* April 28, 1996). Their concern is similar to that of the natives of the Hawaiian island of Maui, where subdivision development on the eastern half destroys agricultural land, ocean access trails, and cultural sites (*Haleaku Times,* April 3–16, 1996). The county of Salt Lake, Utah, is overwhelmed with development proposals resulting from annual growth rates of fifteen to twenty percent and the urbanization of historically rural frontier areas where residents cherish the absence of regulation (*Desert News,* Web edition, April 21, 1996).

In Huntsville, Alabama, residents consider regulations which protect downslope property owners from the construction practices of their upslope neighbors (*Virtual Times,* Huntsville edition, May 2, 1996). The City of Woodside, California, struggles with the question of how to rein in nouveau riche entrepreneurs intent on building residential palaces that double as corporate retreats (*New York Times,* February 18, 1996). Citizens throughout the country look for ways to control the proliferation of cellular towers while phone companies claim that local zoning powers are limited by the Federal Communications Act of 1996.

Each of the development proposals which underlie these stories will, if implemented, change the character and quality of life within a community. First, however, each proposal will be subject to public hearings that will determine government action or inaction. In many cases, public hearings represent citizens' last practical opportunity to shape the future of their communities. Hearings, then, are critical.

On average, people are willing to invest up to thirty percent of their lifelong income in their living environment. And business people invest a substantial part of their net worth in the expectation that a given business location will maintain its viability and not be threatened by incompatible development. The most important investment which people make is in their homes, businesses, and communities.

Battles over land use are perhaps not as much battles against growth and change as they are battles for preserva-

A RIGHT OR A BELIEF?

Since *Village of Euclid vs. Amber Realty Company,* decided in 1926, the U.S. Supreme Court has consistently recognized the legitimate right of government to legislate land use for the protection of the public welfare. In exercising this right, the government cannot deprive a property owner of all reasonable economic use of his property, nor can it act arbitrarily, using the law to accomplish against an individual property owner what it is otherwise unable or unwilling to do through direct compensation. However, as a matter of constitutional law, the government has a broad ability to mitigate the public impact of private development. This is an authority which has been used to uphold laws mandating historic preservation, wetlands protection, pollution control, zoning, signage restriction, aesthetic regulation, and impact fee and required dedication ordinances. Euclid is still the law today. The government cannot single out individual property owners, nor can it act in an arbitrary manner. The ends must justify the means. Despite all this, the debate over private rights in this country tends to center on philosophy and vision rather than law and authority.

tion of rights and public benefits. Change is a constant. It is inevitable. But the public has a right to expect that when development does occur, it will be rational in relationship to its surroundings. We expect development to retain context, keeping in mind the existing landscape as well as competing uses of scarce and often public resources.

The public also has a right to expect that the public benefits of non-development, or of development with conditions, may often outweigh individual economic interests. Preservation of historic structures, or natural resources and habitats such as forests, beaches, and wetlands, may supersede an individual or corporate interest in their destruction. Inclusion of landscaping, lighting, drainage, buffering, sidewalks, and public spaces may be necessary to ameliorate the public impact of a specific development proposal. The public also has a right to expect that development decisions will withstand the test of time. Will the development serve not only present but also future public needs?

In Hermosa Beach, California, a community just north of Los Angeles, the State of California and City of Hermosa Beach are grappling with the proposed construction of an oil derrick—just five blocks off shore. (*San Francisco Chronicle,* June 12, 1998). Through the employment of a new drilling technology known as "slant drilling" rigs like the one proposed are able to drill horizontally to reach points far offshore from near shore locations. Can you imagine having built your home on the coast or being an avid user of the public beach and having an oil derrick then located in your scenic view? Will a decision to allow the construction of the derrick withstand the test of time—or would such a decision represent short term thinking, sacrificing future public needs for current economic gain?

We rely largely on government to ask and answer these hard questions. We rely on government regulation and decision-making to protect our quality of life and our investments from unexpected and incompatible development. When an agency or legislative arm of government responsible for rational land use policy fails in its mission, or when the public fails to oppose noncontextual development effectively, the results are often catastrophic. Short-sighted decisions can destroy communities, quality of life, and citizens' livelihoods, and can incur enormous public cost down the road. Such decisions may be politically expedient, but they are intellectually bankrupt.

It is in the eye of the beholder whether a given development choice is defined as poor, noncontextual, or not in the best interest of a neighborhood or community. What is appropriate in Muskegon, Michigan, may be inappropriate in Naples, Florida, and vice versa. What is acceptable to the community of Crosswicks, New Jersey, may not be consistent with the vision of Bend, Oregon. Each community and neighborhood must develop its own vision of what is appropriate.

Often the vision is not well defined. It evolves as decisions accumulate in response to the many development proposals that each community must face. Rarely are all proposals acceptable to all citizens.

In New York City, not all share the popular vision of Mayor Rudolph W. Giuliani that the Times Square neighborhood is better off free of adult use establishments. In San Francisco, not all agree with local legislation designed to free street right of ways from an explosion of multi colored newspaper boxes in favor of pedestal systems which house all publications in a neatly organized one color structure.

The clash between proposals and community vision is what land use conflict is all about, and how it is resolved affects our quality of life in a real sense. Yet too often the average citizen has only a vague idea of how to challenge proposals that would result in noncontextual development or inappropriate use of scarce public resources.

Conflicts take three general forms, depending upon the participants. First is the conflict initiated by the government body, for example, when it proposes a public works project or use of publicly owned land. Second is the conflict arising when a developer makes a proposal that would affect the community. Third is the conflict of neighbor versus neighbor, whether in a residential, commercial, agricultural, or industrial setting.

In the following chapters, I will refer to the advocate of a given development choice as the *proponent*. The proponent may be a neighbor, developer, or government agency. The party opposing the development choice will be called the *opponent* or *opposition*. This may be a neighbor, neighborhood association, ad hoc group, or any number of other organizations. Proponents and opponents share the stage with *decisionmakers,* that is, members of local, state, and federal boards and agencies charged with exercising discretion in public hearings. Professionals employed by the government to provide technical support and recommendations, hereafter referred to as *staff,* also play important roles in most land use disputes.

An example of the first form of conflict, that initiated by a government agency, is when a municipality proposes the construction of an expressway, a landfill, or a sewage treatment plant in a community. Or the local government body may dictate the use of publicly held property for a purpose that undermines adjacent areas. Parks and municipal stadiums often fall into this category.

The second type of conflict, developer initiated, is in the news every day. The developer may be a utility that wants to build a dam to the detriment of a fishery. The developer may be a builder who proposes a subdivision with a slash and burn policy that would destroy native habitats just outside someone's back door. Or the developer may be a company proposing a mall that would turn local neighborhood streets into six and eight lane thoroughfares. These asphalt rivers discourage community socialization and often put an end to pedestrian and bicycle traffic, an important component of neighborhood security.

The final type of conflict, neighbor versus neighbor, is increasingly common. In this conflict, each property owner becomes a mini-developer grabbing everything he or she can get that is not already withheld by deed restrictions, regulations, and ordinances. The inevitable result is depreciation of property value and more subtly, loss of sense of place. People have an intuitive need for familiar surroundings, security, and a sense of belonging to a community. All these can bring peace of mind. When change is proposed that threatens the fabric and tranquillity of a community, the residents lose their sense of place, a result which transcends all forms of land use conflict.

Often the offending neighbor has a singular goal of squeezing every bit of value from external amenities such as mountain or water views. Striving for the "bigger castle," these mini-developers adopt their own on-site slash and burn programs, positioning their buildings to maximize views without considering the effect upon neighbors.

Many mountain communities like Aspen, Colorado, repeatedly grapple with a balancing of equities between those who have built their dream homes and those who wish to build the next palace, bigger, better, higher. Local planning boards strive to attain aesthetic standards that will make ten-thousand-square-foot homes blend in with mountain ridges while not obstructing the views of others. Aspen shares this challenge with Santa Fe, where trophy homes proliferate on mountain slopes. Each of these communities would like to retain the pristine nature which makes it unique. But development of the mountain ridges is a hard reality.

In transitional neighborhoods such as Vanderbilt Beach, Florida, a coastal waterfront community, it is not uncommon to find four-story palatial homes with first-floor elevations beginning at the eves of a neighboring home built several years earlier. These noncontextual designs obstruct neighbors' views, thereby destroying their sense of place and their property values.

Sometimes the offensive neighbor is the government itself. Public facilities such as schools, fire stations, landfills, and public stadiums generate noise, odors, light, and traffic which inevitably affect neighbors. Balancing the interests of neighbors and the public as a whole is often one of government's biggest challenges.

Government bodies have the unique ability to affect land use through failure to regulate or to enforce existing regulations. Jim Kuch, a biology teacher living in Muskegon, Michigan, learned this the hard way. Mr. Kuch built a cabin on a five-acre tract in a densely wooded area filled with deer and other wildlife. The site was a short walk from Lake Michigan where deer would water. Given the size of his parcel and the character of the area, Mr. Kuch believed that he would be able to enjoy the natural environment of his land. A rogue developer purchased an adjacent tract and immediately constructed a barbed-wire fence through the woods. The fence prevents any deer or other wildlife from traversing Mr. Kuch's property on the way to the lake. This simple conflict arose because an archaic township ordinance forbidding such fences was generally not enforced.

The neighbor versus neighbor conflict often extends into areas zoned for agricultural, commercial, and industrial uses, where some of the most insensitive development proposals occur. There is the farmer who insists upon removing vegetation that stabilizes a riverbank, accelerating erosion, damaging fisheries, or curbing enjoyment of the resource for downstream neighbors. There is the funeral home operator who insists on building next to a restaurant hotel in a tourist district. There is the industrial spray paint facility located next to the car lot.

Occasionally, the conflict is highly unusual. Take a case reported by the *New York Times* (March 10, 1996) pitting surfers, abalone fishermen, and environmental groups against charter boat captains. According to the story, the charter boat captains were chumming the waters in the Monterey Bay Marine Sanctuary off the coast of California in the hopes of attracting great white sharks so that tourists could see them. Surfers who frequent the sanctuary and consider themselves comparatively low on the food

DIMINIMUS, OR LACK OF JURISDICTION

Many state and federal statutes do not extend their reach to small parcels or petitions which are below threshold levels of development. State and federal governments, or their agencies, may also determine that a certain development project, though it affects a broader ecosystem, are nonetheless subject to the exclusive application of local ordinances. This is what is meant by diminimus, or lack of jurisdiction. The irony is that the cumulative impact of the exceptions often defeats the underlying purposes of broader regulatory schemes. Ecosystems die a slow death, parcel by development parcel.

chain concluded that chumming was a threat. At the request of the surfers, divers, and conservation organizations, the National Oceanic and Atmospheric Administration has now proposed rules to ban the chumming.

Land use conflicts have become more numerous and intense for many reasons, notably diminishing natural resources, vanishing open space, and increasing development pressure. Historically, intensive use of land, while perhaps degrading to the environment or community, was often isolated and thus tolerated. Today, in an increasingly congested world, people are recognizing that each use of land (or sea) affects neighboring property owners and the rights of the public.

Traditionally, of course, Americans have embraced growth and viewed it as dependent upon the exploitation of cheap abundant resources and the defoliation of real property—the removal of every tree, the excavation of all minerals, the filling of all wetlands. We Americans have tended to engineer our environment rather than try to understand it and plan for its future. Construction is progress. Progress is jobs. Some are beginning to see preservation and rational development as growth industries with the potential to create jobs and opportunity, but we are still caught in a tangle of competing philosophies. When development proposals are first laid on the table, they meet with varied local responses depending on which competing value predominates at the time.

Often development proceeds with little or no public scrutiny. Property may be zoned for uses which, though incompatible or out of context with their surroundings, are nonetheless allowed by local ordinance. In some cases, too, proposed uses also may not trigger application of state or federal statutes because of their *diminimus* nature which causes a lack of jurisdiction. Affected neighbors or communities then have to buttress their case by arguing for their own private property rights or depend on the benevolence of the proponent—neither a comforting thought.

More often, proposals proceed through a public process. At the local level this may be zoning, comprehensive plan, or a site plan review. At the state or federal level, this may require that the proponent obtain permits in such areas as water use or land management.

Virtually all land use conflicts are aired in one or more public hearings that ultimately determine the fate of the development proposal. These dramas play themselves out in meeting halls and through the print and broadcast media from coast to coast. While there are many variations on the script, the issues involved and the way decisions are made are remarkably similar.

Most citizens are at a marked disadvantage in understanding how to challenge inappropriate development proposals. Much development proceeds not on its own merits, but for lack of challenge. Too often, objections are not voiced until the spade hits the dirt and it is too late.

How can you stage a challenge to protect your home, business, or community from development that threatens your quality of life or your investment? Before we move on to that subject, a caveat: If you plan to oppose development, or a particular form of it, you are better off *not* adopting a strategy of manipulation. To launch a successful campaign, you have to think and act not deceptively, but rather strategically. You have to summon the heart to win.

CHAPTER 2

The Power of Prevention

*E**arly*** in their ordeal, citizens challenging a development proposal will likely ask the question—How did we get here? The answer, often, is that they allowed their communities to become complacent about the possibility of incompatible development. Collective apathy requires less short term effort than a course of vigilance and citizen involvement.

Why is it important for communities and neighborhoods to overcome collective apathy? How do they strengthen themselves?

The answer to the first question is simple. Politicians, developers, builders, and architects don't pick on strong neighborhoods that expect and understand the meaning of rational development. Proponents of irrational development take the path of least resistance, gravitating toward communities with the weakest defenses. Strong communities, communities which have a keen awareness of their surroundings and prospective development, generally endure less conflict.

The answer to the second question is more involved. Strong communities don't just exist; like athletes they go through a long, hard, regimen of training. It takes time, commitment, and perseverance to create a strong community. Four elements are vital:

Planning

Community responsibility

Community associations

Communication among citizens

PLANNING

Like individuals, communities and neighborhoods benefit from a strong sense of identity and vision. They must have community goals and a plan to implement them.

The American landscape reflects many types of planning. On one end of the spectrum is the community that dismisses planning as a meaningless bureaucratic exercise. On the other end is the neighborhood that plots its future in intricate detail. Most places fall somewhere between the two extremes.

A developer who invades comparatively inexpensive agricultural land, surveys the back forty into sixteen two-and-a-half-acre tracts, obtains a survey, records a plat, and builds an isolated subdivision is a classic symptom of the unplanned community. How will sewers and water be extended to the community? Where will the new children go to school? Will the community pay its fair share for needs it has created, such as roads and utilities? And will the community be logical in relationship to what surrounds it?

This type of isolated subdivision is prevalent throughout America. It is urban development in a rural setting, allowed without a plan. One day the residents of the community will pay a price for their lack of planning, for it will weaken the neighborhood and make it susceptible to development proposals exhibiting the same absence of foresight that resulted in the construction of the isolated subdivision in the first place.

Some communities just won't plan. Ironically, those that most value property rights and rugged individualism, and thus are most likely to view planners as the ultimate government bureaucrats, are the very communities that development proponents are hungry for. Dogged allegiance to the rubric of property rights may well destroy the community fabric which citizens so strongly cherish. Ranching and farming communities that fail to protect themselves against encroaching development may be passively undermining their way of life in the name of tough individualism.

At the other end of the spectrum is the planned community that regulates all the way down to the color and type of mailbox an owner can buy. Such communities often do anticipate and provide for future needs, like water, sanitary sewer, internal roads, water management, lighting, and utilities. They pay impact fees for schools, parks, and other public infrastructure that will be required to serve the broader community. But are they always strong? Not always. Though the community may be well planned internally, it may not relate well to adjacent communities. Therein lies another irony. Even though a neighborhood may be internally planned, if its relationship to surrounding communities is taken into consideration, it may end up being just another isolated spot on the map.

A good example of the planned but weak community is the walled development. Walling off creates a fortress or island mentality that inhibits communication with surrounding areas. Walled communities often find themselves subject to some of the worst development decisions because they are unable to develop strategic alliances with neighboring communities on major development proposals.

Again, most communities lie between these extremes. They implement intermediate levels of planning with some fairly detailed zoning regulation, which is enforced, and provision for comprehensive or master planning. Though these communities may not always be as aesthetically pleasing as planned communities, they can be strong. They have the mechanisms in place to control development through public debate. Their fate is their own.

Planning is not always effective. Despite the best of intentions, some communities lose their character because they plan without adequate resources or public support. It may be that community planners lack the skills required to execute the articulated public vision. Keep in mind also that planning is not a static process. As the vision changes, community plans must be evaluated over and over again. Many communities spend thousands of dollars and countless hours on a plan only to put it on the shelf and forget about it. There is no plan for implementing the plan!

COMMUNITY RESPONSIBILITY

Civic responsibility is also critical to the strength of community. Citizens who spend hours of their free time trying to make their community a better place to live view themselves as part of a whole. They understand that their neighborhoods will survive only with their participation. And they know that participation cannot be left to others. At the same time they recognize that the well being of the community is in their individual interest.

Strength builds from the bottom up. Where there is a sense of responsibility towards the neighborhood, there is a sense of responsibility towards the larger community. Communities cannot be strong without strong neighborhoods. Allow me to return to the example of the walled neighborhood. Citizens who live behind walls in the search for security, live behind front doors as well. Isolated, they don't always, or even usually, view themselves as beholden to the neighborhood. Their responsibility is paying association dues for turn key services. The neighborhood is there to serve them. They are not there to serve the neighborhood.

Communities that become a collection of gated neighborhoods are geographic islands. They are invariably weak. There is a limited sense of community responsibility because there is a limited sense of neighborhood responsibility. Citizens pay their dues, they pay their taxes, and everything else is supposed to take care of itself. Communities without a strong ethic of community responsibility are bright red targets for proponents of poor development choices. Proponents know that when the alarm sounds, there will be no response.

COMMUNITY ASSOCIATIONS

Another element of community strength is presence in the form of citizen associations. Such associations make themselves felt in many ways, including public objection to development activities which are inconsistent with community standards. Citizens have to be vigilant. They can't depend on overworked, under-budgeted government officials to blow the whistle when the wolf is at the door. If development standards exist but aren't enforced, it will only encourage additional development which doesn't meet the standards. Why should developers expect to be subject to standards that are not applied to others?

STRENGTH IN NUMBERS

The number of homeowner associations in the United States:

1964	Fewer than 500
1970	10,000
1975	20,000
1980	55,000
1990	130,000
1992	150,000
2000	225,000 (projected)

The 150,000 associations in 1992 governed 32 million people and were split among regions as follows:

West	36%
South	33%
Northeast	21%
Midwest	10%

(Evan McKenzie, *Privatopia: Homeowner Associations and the rise of Residential Private Government*, New Haven: Yale Univ. Press, 1994, p.11, 20 and n.74)

Blowing the whistle isn't all. Associations might work to maintain community amenities such as entry statements, street signs, landscaping, and lighting that provide a sense of place. These signal to the entire community that residents take great pride in living there.

In 1989 Vanderbilt Beach, Florida, a community of approximately 800 single-family, 800 multi-family, and 25 commercial gulf-front businesses, had no sense of place. The neighborhood had over 110 newspaper boxes scattered throughout the right of way, which inhibited landscaping. The street signs, the same ones the original developer had put in during the 1960s, were badly weathered. Fewer than 200 members belonged to a voluntary property owners association, and it rarely involved itself in community affairs. The message to the community was that the area did not act as a neighborhood. The results were predictable. There was a lack of funding for road improvements. Developers routinely ignored the deed restrictions by building multi-family duplexes in single-family areas. Neighborhood opinions were largely ignored in comprehensive planning. The area was fair game for all.

In the late 1980s Art Jacob, retired president of the National Shoe Salesmen of America, was recruited as president of the neighborhood association. Mr. Jacob worked to recruit new leadership and to develop a vision for the neighborhood. Soon a voluntary agreement was entered into with newspaper publishers which placed all of their uniformly colored brown boxes in 3 turnout areas, removed from the right of ways. A group of 25 people from the association replaced all 110 street signs throughout the community with uniformly painted signs having custom-designed logos. Two landscaped entries were built and maintained, letting people know that they were entering a neighborhood.

Today the Vanderbilt Beach Property Owners Association has a constant presence on various county advisory boards and at county commission meetings. The membership has tripled to over six hundred, and monthly general membership meetings attract over seventy persons. The area has enacted traffic calming measures and, with the support of the county government, completed a one-and-a-half-mile beach renourishment project. The association entered into a testing program with two conservancy organizations, the Nature Conservancy of Southwest Florida and the Wiggins Pass Conservancy, in an effort to preserve water quality.

Presence empowers the neighborhood of Vanderbilt Beach. The county commission considers its views because the neighborhood association is viewed as representative. Developers routinely call to ask for an audience before acting. Other neighborhood associations align themselves with the Vanderbilt Beach

Property Owners Association on many key development issues. County staff members provide the association leadership with advance notice of proposed developments.

COMMUNICATION AMONG CITIZENS

Finally, communication is the lifeblood of a strong community. Many who would otherwise participate in community discussions are often not aware of development proposals unless there is an effective means of communication. Most citizens simply don't have the time to keep abreast of community issues outside of what they might read in the local newspaper.

Meanwhile, developers have highly skilled professionals keeping them up to date on unfolding community issues and planning efforts. They have a one-hundred-yard head start in a two-hundred-yard race to the approval finish line. The politicians, developers, and architects/builders must know that you as a community will be aware of development proposals early in the development process. This will encourage them to come to the association first, before they are too committed to development plans that may or may not be acceptable to the community.

How is communication maintained? The newsletter is one way. Issued at predictable intervals, it keeps neighborhood members aware of local events and lets them know that the association is working in their best interests. Another way is a highly active network of board members who stay informed and keep each other informed.

Then there is the trusty phone. Telephone trees can be extremely effective. One person calls four people, each of whom call four more and so on, until the entire community is saturated with the news of late-breaking developments.

Innovative communities are learning to use electronic communication through the Internet. They post Web pages and e-mail to bring all members of the community up to date instantaneously. Once it is fully understood and widely used, the Internet will level the playing field in land use conflicts and help promote strong communities. This may be especially helpful in second home or resort communities where development proposals are approved in the off-season. Neighbors will be instantaneously informed regardless of where they are.

Planning, civic responsibility, organized associations, and communication among citizens create strong communities. And strong communities are the primary means of keeping development proposals from unfolding into major conflicts. In a strong community many inappropriate proposals will never see the light of day. In a weak community, there will be ongoing public warfare generated by fully developed proposals surfacing at the proverbial eleventh hour or, in the worst case, after the concrete is in the ground.

Part 2

A PLAN OF ACTION

CHAPTER 3

The Heart to Win

When the trumpet blares a warning about an onrushing development proposal, each citizen potentially affected by it makes a personal choice: should I get involved? It is a question to be answered with great care, for the process of challenging development is draining, emotional, and time consuming. It takes away from family and friends. It costs money. It puts opponents at the mercy of those who control the timing of hearings and events.

Each citizen's priorities are different. The decision to get involved is not for everyone. This is the rule that should prevail: if both your head and heart are fully committed, participate. If not, don't, for then you will be raising expectations you cannot fulfill. Remember, however, that if enough citizens do not choose a course of opposition, development will proceed unchallenged. Showing up is a manner of voting. If nobody shows up, nobody votes.

Why do citizens avoid participation? They may not believe that they can succeed. Or they may see their opportunity cost (time away from work and family) as exceeding the likely gain from involvement. Or it may just be that they are collectively apathetic.

Citizens recognize the roadblocks to opposition. They understand that proponents have a head start, that development proposals often need a running start to come to fruition. They know that sometimes months, or even years, of groundwork are established before a proposal enters the arena of public discussion. Citizens understand that the proponents hire savvy professionals to develop the pro arguments before the proposal is ever exposed to the public forum. Moreover, proponents hire top guns because they are confident of success in the first place—otherwise they wouldn't expend so much time and money. Citizens understand, too, that as potential opponents their own resources would be limited. Citizens want to win. They do not buy into efforts destined to lose. They want to use their time productively.

And then there are the opportunity costs. When it comes down to a choice between attending public meetings and just about anything else, anything else is usually going to come first. Association meetings and deliberative meetings before government bodies tend to be long, loud, confused, emotional, uncertain in their outcome, and generally less satisfying than, say, watching the kids' basketball game or taking the spouse to dinner. There is also a financial cost for many. For example, most working adults cannot afford to take the time off from work to attend daytime meetings, regardless of how strongly they may be opposed to a particular development proposal.

Of course, many citizens just don't care. They don't care because they don't understand the danger inherent in many development proposals. Or they believe that all development is good development or that someone else will always carry the responsibility. Whatever the reason for collective apathy, not caring by enough citizens means that the developer lands on Monopoly's Boardwalk.

So some citizens can opt out because of fear of failure, high opportunity costs, or collective apathy. What motivates others—those that do become involved? Most commonly, a group of citizens wakes up to the fact that they have a strong economic stake in the outcome of a development decision.

DEVELOPMENT OF REGIONAL IMPACT

A development of regional impact under Florida law is a development which by size, or intensity, is deemed to be so large that it affects regional resources such as roads, schools, utilities, and other public facilities. Such a development requires both state and local review. Other states have similar requirements for large developments.

Pelican Bay is a three-thousand-unit upscale development of single and multi-family homes bordering the City of Naples in Collier County, Florida. It was the crown jewel of a national development company throughout the 1980s and early 1990s. Pelican Bay was only the second Development of Regional Impact (DRI) approved by the State of Florida, the first being Disney World in Orlando.

Pelican Bay was built within a coastal zone on the boundaries of a pristine mangrove forest and estuary system adjoining the Gulf of Mexico. The estuary was a marketing tool for a dozen high-rise sites located on the boundary of the estuary. High-rise developers would showcase views to potential purchasers that took in all the wonders of the estuary and the gulf and spent millions of dollars marketing these views throughout the United States and abroad. The marketing was wildly successful. It created hundreds of millions of dollars of property value. On the mere basis of a view, buyers paid anywhere from $600,000 to more than $1 million for luxury condominiums.

During development, roads were built that compacted the areas surrounding the mangrove estuary. Several respected scientists believe that this, along with the effects of earlier development, limited the interchange of water between the Gulf of Mexico and the estuary. The area also received above-normal rainfall. Much of the mangrove forest died as trees apparently drowned, although exact causes of the die-off are unknown, or in dispute. The dying forest became a forty-acre testament to poor development. The million dollar views were now marred by dying vegetation.

The situation was enough to galvanize the residents of Pelican Bay. Looking down on a dying mangrove forest is not what they expected when they bought their condominiums. With hundreds of millions of dollars of property value jeopardized, the residents of Pelican Bay have opted to endure the long public meetings until a remedy is found.

Economic motivations extend to rural areas and middle- and lower-income levels as well. For example, residents in rural low income areas have tremendous economic motivation to actively oppose landfills near their homes which may be their only substantial assets.

Citizens also act out of concern for quality of life. An example is reported in the *Raleigh News & Observer* of North Carolina (April 28, 1996). Farmers in the Raleigh region are concerned that rapid development has destroyed over 26% of the farmland in the six-county region between 1978 and 1992. Several of the farmers have placed conservation easements on their property to limit development.

Sometimes citizens engage out of civic pride. Citizen watchdogs watch decisionmakers run their paces over and over. They attend all meetings because they care about their community and are not content to sit on the sidelines. Others get involved when the government, developer, or neighbor hits the wrong button, kicks the sleeping dog. Many citizens don't like to watch other people being arbitrarily deprived of their quality of life. It might one day be them.

Why should you, as a citizen, get involved? The hard reality is that your community and neighborhood need you. There is strength in numbers and every person counts. Moreover, you have unique skills and knowledge that will enhance the ability of your community to make sound decisions. Your participation is a vote.

Because of your involvement, maybe, just maybe, a better choice will be made for the future of your community. Perhaps the choice will withstand the test of time. Or perhaps you won't care, and nobody else will. Nobody will show up. Nobody will vote. Involvement is a personal choice. Are you committed, both head and heart? It's your choice.

Once people decide to get involved, they must join in a strong and efficient group effort. This may take place within the context of an existing civic, neighborhood, or environmental organization. Often it involves multiple organizations. Whichever way opposition energy is channeled, its success depends first on quality leadership, a belief in what the opposition is trying to achieve, and teamwork—in other words, the heart to win.

THE LEADERSHIP

The opposition must have capable leadership if it is to succeed. And capable leadership can be difficult to come by. Why?

Neighbors or members of the opposition group may subject the leader to personal criticism, forgetting that he or she, too, is a volunteer. The leader may become a surrogate for decisionmakers or agency staff when it comes time for citizens to voice their frustration. And the leader often has to compromise, which may be highly unpopular. The leader with a thin skin won't prove effective.

The person who opts to lead the charge has to expect certain disruptions, such as late night phone calls and constant political pressure. The leader must also be willing to accept that his or her schedule will be disrupted. When municipal staff or decisionmakers decide to call special meetings or when journalists phone to discuss development proposals, the person who represents the opposition must be available. That person must also expect to spend large amounts of time preparing the opposition's case.

Ideal opposition leaders are thick skinned and generous with their time. They are also articulate and focused. They clarify the opponent's position, wear emotional Teflon in the heat of debate, and remain sensitive to, but do not define themselves by, what others think, good or bad.

One other point about leadership: the lookout is not the captain. The civic-minded watchdog who spotted the problem or who is the most vocal member of the opposition isn't necessarily best equipped to lead the charge. Leaders must be capable of reasoning, not merely emoting. Leaders must make many strategic decisions, and informed decisions are best made with careful analysis, not emotional rhetoric.

In identifying an effective leader, search for the articulate, fearless soul who can be empathetic but who also has a sense of humor. The leader must be proficient in running meetings, setting the agenda, establishing priorities, and making sure that individual views receive a fair hearing, including the obligatory venting. The leader must be able to forge consensus. In other words, opposition leaders must have superior political skills. In fact, they often serve in a political capacity after the purpose of the opposition has been served, win or lose.

There is a natural tendency in land use situations to select leaders with certain skills from within the community, for instance, resident lawyers, planners, architects, and former business executives. To be effective as leaders they must be able to divorce themselves from their professional biases. Their personal vision may well not be the community vision.

I live in Vanderbilt Beach, Florida, and was president of the Vanderbilt Beach Property Owners Association from 1993 through January 1997. Our leadership, together with the leadership of an adjoining neighborhood, Naples Park, was able to persuade Collier County to install stop signs on a local road, Vanderbilt Drive, which was quickly being transformed into a short cut for through traffic between communities to the north and south. The through traffic was destroying the character of the two neighborhoods. The stop signs immediately calmed traffic, redirecting much of it back to major arterials. The neighborhoods on Vanderbilt Drive became safer, which encouraged pedestrian use of the right of way.

Subsequently, a local planner who happened to be a resident of Naples Park promoted the idea of removing the stop signs and constructing traffic circles. That was his bias, one that I shared. However, the community as a whole opposed the idea and so it wasn't pursued. Our leadership positions compelled us to give up our personal agendas.

THE TEAM

Once you have identified the quarterback, you must make sure that there is team conviction. The team that doesn't believe in itself cannot score. It isn't uncommon for an opposition group to become enraptured with its mission, to place an article in the local paper, putting the leader out on a limb, and then as the going gets tough to abandon the cause. Pity the leader! It is probably the last time that brave but publicly embarrassed person will ever step up to bat.

In the 1960s anthem "Alice's Restaurant," Arlo Guthrie used a poignant line to motivate thousands of Americans to protest the draft. If just one person sang "Alice's Restaurant," the draft board would think he was crazy, but if several people joined in it would be viewed as a movement. Agree or disagree with Guthrie's political views, he had a point. There is strength in numbers.

When intrusive development looms, energizing the opposition is a tremendous challenge. Taking critical conversation from the kitchen table to the bargaining table is the American exception, not the rule. It is easier to bond as victims at the local church, country club, or neighborhood bar than it is to bond by action in local meeting halls. Action requires ongoing commitment, and it is much easier for most people to listen to themselves complain.

The world tends to accept you on your own terms. If your opposition group doesn't have the conviction to mount an organized effort, don't expect the public or decisionmakers to view your opposition as important. If you won't make the emotional investment to consider alternative approaches to confronting proposed development, don't expect more of anyone else.

Coordination is also critical to the team's effectiveness. Rarely will one person possess all the skills needed to challenge a development proposal. Every member of the team should have a role, and it should match that person's skills. No one should try to do it all. When the call of all hands on deck goes out, there should be a captain, a communications officer, a media coordinator, one or more detectives, and a negotiator.

Establishing teamwork can be difficult, especially at the outset of the opposition effort. Members may not understand each other's talents. Even when discrepancies in skills are apparent, there is often reluctance to challenge volunteered resources. Strong neighborhood organizations often minimize this problem. Fellow members who have been through the wars together will have an understanding of each others' strengths and weaknesses. Also, if the opposition survives the initial stages of battle, it will have an opportunity to adjust roles and to practice teamwork before the final verdict is delivered.

There is also an emotional side to the teamwork equation. Members must resist the tendency for the opposition process to become an end in itself. Because the stakes are high and the participants unfamiliar, and because there is an enemy or target in the proponent of the development, opposition can easily become a personal proving ground for individual agendas, a test track, or a means of satisfying individual needs for attention. Land use challenge requires strategic thinking if it is to succeed. Emotional interference clouds objectives and breaks down coordination among members of the opposition.

You are on a mission. You face obstacles, perhaps daunting odds. You must be tactical, committed, and coordinated in all of your efforts. Above all, you must speak with one voice. Emotional volleyball diminishes your ability to do any or all of these things. Your group is in danger of playing this game under the following conditions:

1. *No Clearly Defined Agenda, or Multiple or Personal Agendas*

If members are debating the agenda after the opposition effort is well under way, it will pull the group in different directions. There is also a danger that, once the group agenda has been established, members will use the visibility of the opposition to promote different agendas, perhaps personal ones.

An example: A member of the opposition, not the chosen leader, wants to run for county commission or city council against the incumbent. He hopes to advance his prospects by demonstrating that the incumbent is ineffectual in addressing development choices. Yet the opposition needs the help and understanding of the incumbent, who is a decisionmaker. The personal agenda is directly contrary to the group agenda.

2. Historical Animosity of Leaders

Conflicting personalities often define group dynamics. Assume that the current president of a neighborhood organization has difficulty relating to the president of the neighborhood association next door, even though their interests are nearly identical. Then a municipal staff member (perhaps sensing the discord) proposes that a local road bordering both neighborhoods be turned into a major collector road, thus increasing capacity and traffic. Assume further that the respective presidents decide to use the resulting debate to revisit old wars. To the decisionmaker, it appears as if the proposed development is not important enough for the leaders to set aside their differences. They probably both lose. Neither wants the enlarged road, but their respective neighborhoods end up with it because they can't take off the boxing gloves.

3. Presence of Monster Egos

The monster ego, a self-proclaimed authority on all topics, advances a personal agenda unrelated to the development proposal. Monster egos are the ultimate torpedo to opposition because they discourage participation by other capable people.

The monster ego may have occupied a position of power in another realm. Naturally, this personality feels confident in the face of challenge, but he or she is likely to be insensitive to group dynamics. After all, the monster ego is used to giving and making decisions. Now, with time to waste, this person is going to experiment with the opposition effort. Perhaps he or she will find some emotional fulfillment in the process. How do you ask a person who is so obviously skilled to follow instead of lead?

Retired attorneys from someplace else are among the worst offenders. They are drafted for their supposed talent in leading op-

The Monster Ego

position to undesirable proposals. Regrettably, they are often wrong for the job. Used to success in a legal field where the rules were different than in the context of land use planning, they are determined to show the proponent and the opposition that their advocacy skills are as sharp as ever.

Monster egos are the kiss of death. In a business environment you would simply fire such people. But because the opposition effort is volunteer, you must find a way to work with them, to use both their skills and commitment in a positive way.

4. Presence of Nitpickers

Many citizens gravitate to opposition groups because they are an outlet to complain. Opposition becomes an extension of their personalities, cynical and untrusting. They tend to be critical of motivations, regardless of how pure, and to manipulate opinion for no apparent purpose. I refer to these citizens as nitpickers. Nitpickers raise their stock by lowering that of others, including the leadership. To nitpickers, actual achievement is marginally important. Being exposed to nitpickers is one of the most prevalent disincentives to public involvement. But every group has at least one.

The presence of one or more of these four conditions should be a warning flag. Members of the opposition will be distracted by the emotional side of the process, endangering their chances of success. Theirs must be a team effort.

And it must be undertaken with full dedication. Having one foot in and one foot out won't work. Dedication bears an inverse relationship to opportunity cost. Let me share an extreme example. There is a virus prevalent in resort communities variously known as beach, mountain, or ranch fever. It refers to the urge of outsiders to buy second homes in paradise. On a visit, they take in the water, mountains, clean air, and open spaces and visualize what it would be like to live there. It becomes their dream. The afflicted make a decision they would never make in business—they buy. The house, condominium, chalet, cabin, ranch, or beach house is theirs. Spontaneous buying signals a commitment to the dream. They are not to be deprived!

Such spontaneous decisions are virtually always made on the basis of a developer's marketing of view and open space. What you see is what you get, until the developer or some successor is forced by economic circumstance to change the plan upon which the dream rested. The developer hopes to exercise the virtually unlimited discretion granted to it under master documents or some other form of reservation by modifying the land plan, perhaps locating condominium, office, or commercial development directly next to the new resident's slice of paradise.

Paradise Lost

The view is gone. Privacy is shot. Wild animals have been scared off. The marketing people told the buyer that it would never happen, and after all, the developer would protect them against noncontextual development using those powers reserved to it under the master documents. The shield becomes the sword.

The new residents have come to relax, vacation, or retire, not to fight lawsuits or attend public meetings in heated opposition to a development proposal on foreign turf with foreign politics. They are the victims. Unwittingly, they placed themselves in the path of development abuse and will probably lose a substantial portion of their investment. Why? Because when the time comes to oppose the plan modification, the collective opportunity cost to the community is so high that members will likely not summon the dedication to rally against it. How quickly paradise loses its glitter.

If you catch the fever, remember that you, like your fellow citizens, must be prepared to muster the dedication to protect the value of your investment and the integrity of your community against looming development proposals.

THE HEART TO WIN

What it all comes down to, in the end, is whether members of the opposition have the heart to win. Opposing development is hard work. It involves many people, sometimes even decisionmakers, with limited skills. And opponents are often underfinanced and overmatched by the developer's resources. Public debate is highly charged and at times seems pointless. Lasting victories are hard to come by.

The heart to win is the intangible quality of perseverance. The road of opposition is planted with obstacles. Understanding this fact and fortifying yourself for the inevitable dips and turns in the decision-making process are essential to surviving and seeing the process through to conclusion. From beginning to end, each opponent must have the heart to win. With leadership, conviction, and dedicated teamwork, your group will be prepared to take on the most challenging of development proposals.

CHAPTER 4

Strategic Thinking

You read in this morning's paper that the owner of the mall adjacent to your neighborhood is planning to double its size, or that the local airport authority is going to consider allowing commercial jet service with the flight path directly over your home, or that the county commission is considering a proposal to allow segmented breakwaters in a natural channel or pass that would block safe passage, or that local churches want to open a soup kitchen next to your retirement neighborhood, or that the county proposes to discharge storm water directly into the intercostal waterway where you live, or that a prominent and well-funded developer hopes to build a twenty-two-story luxury condominium on the fringe of an estuary in which you regularly canoe and fish.

The offending proposal has gathered a head of steam. The developer has the plans and professionals lined up, has fully lobbied the decisionmakers, fully analyzed and prepared its strategy, and believes that it has a reasonable chance of success. The developer has the green light.

The council or commission is made up of new members. The manager, who believes this is a beneficial public project, has directed staff to let the project proceed. You thought the project was dead; it was rejected by the prior board. Now you are in the position of having to fight the fight all over again.

The community early-warning system has failed, and your voluntary neighborhood association recently experienced a change of leadership. Or, if you are in a resort community, the proposal is advancing during the holiday or off-season. It will be almost impossible to motivate a crowd to attend a hearing, but you may be able to count on a few of the diehard watchdogs. The developer knew that. The manager knew that too, but discounted it, for business must be conducted.

What do you do? What does your community do? There is a general feeling, shared by your neighbors, that you will follow American tradition and go down to city hall or the county seat and have a talk with the elected officials or manager. As you soon discover, a number of development professionals have been there first and the staff has committed to a report favorable to the proposal, already written and submitted. Several elected officials have now appeared on the local radio talk show speaking in favor of the proposal, prior to the hearing.

Certainly the elected officials will see the common sense of your opposition. You will attend the meeting with the diehards and try to derail the runaway locomotive. But down inside, you have the sinking feeling that either you are overmatched or you have been pre-empted—the decisions have been made and the hearings are a formality.

This series of events is the rule rather than the exception for critical development proposals. The conflict is on. Fight or flight—that is your choice.

The only way to challenge such proposals is with *strategic thinking*. With it, you have a chance. Without it, you can start planning for how you will rearrange your life when the developer's trucks start rolling in.

Strategic thinking begins with the formation of a strong, dedicated opposition group. The group then identifies its goals and adopts a strategy for their achievement. In developing strategy, the opposition group sets the tone for community discussion.

Often citizen groups define their objectives and strategy in very narrow terms. They fight the question "whether" rather than of "how" and "when."

Let's say that a local municipality proposes a road through your neighborhood which will bring additional development and traffic through what historically has been a peaceful and quiet community. A quick community reaction and strategy might be to fight the construction of the road in any form. And in given cases, that may be the appropriate strategy.

However, does that solve the problem? Is the problem of the public need for the road going to go away? In several states the construction of roads is driven by a doctrine called concurrency— state mandated funding and construction on the basis of projected populations and level-of-service models. Notwithstanding the doctrine's obviously flawed assumptions, it may be the law.

Perhaps the most important question is not whether the proposed road should be built. Perhaps the most important questions are how and when. There are many ways to build a road.

Will the road merely reflect slash and burn development, exclusively designed to move traffic at the highest possible speeds from point A to point B regardless of what happens to the neighborhood? Or will it relate to the neighborhood and enhance the security of its citizens? Will the road be friendly to pedes-

CONCURRENCY

Concurrency is a doctrine adopted by the State of Florida which, by law, requires local governments to build roads before projected growth takes place. The practical result of this requirement is that road construction creates the very growth it was intended to serve. New roads are built for theoretical subdivisions. Existing roads are widened. The underlying assumption of concurrency is that moving more traffic at higher speeds by laying more asphalt better represents community priorities than moving less traffic at lower speeds and having quieter, safer, and more pedestrian-friendly neighborhoods. The fear of two-lane traffic jams becomes the reality of six-lane parking lots separating neighborhoods and dividing different parts of whole communities.

trians, bicyclists, and joggers with sidewalks and bike paths? Will it include median and right-of-way landscaping to improve appearance? Entry signs that serve as a signature for the community?

Might the road be designed with traffic-calming measures such as roundabouts, narrow lanes, medians, and edge striping, so that traffic moves slowly and the road does not become a race track? What about the possible location of shelters and benches at school stops for children? Will the road design incorporate lighting from which adjacent residential properties are shielded by means of glare control devices? Will it provide refuges for pedestrians?

Is the community ready to say yes to these questions? Or can decisionmakers be persuaded to delay construction until the community is able to afford such measures? This raises the next question: when?

Perhaps construction of the road is inevitable, and in the greater interest of the community. Perhaps a decision against construction will ultimately be a Pyrrhic victory. The community will receive a strictly utilitarian design in the future rather than a contextual design today. It might be better to concede to construction while requiring it to meet the highest community standards.

That is not to say that there are not times when the question should be whether. Specifically in cases involving the destruction of nonrenewable resources and habitats, this question may define planning for both us and future generations. But in all cases, opponents must decide which question deserves the greater commitment of time and effort when they are forming their strategy.

Timing is a critical part of strategy. Making agreements with proponents financially equipped to bring about development solutions is often preferable to waiting for another proponent who may not have the financial ability or be willing to make the same commitments. What might be achieved today may not necessarily be achieved tomorrow.

In the case of the government proponent (as opposed to the developer), the rule on timing is simple and often overlooked. The appropriate time to address the question "how" is when government is budgeting for public improvements.

Citizen opposition groups often surface when construction is imminent. At that point, budgets are set and government units have virtually no power to enhance utilitarian designs. Everything will be done on the cheap. Neighborhoods will receive utilitarian designs regardless of how badly decisionmakers may wish they had made different decisions. They just won't have the money.

However, if community groups voice objections during the annual budgetary process, they will control the purse strings. It is far easier to include recreational and safety components at this stage because the decisionmakers will just factor them into the overall cost. And if the choice comes down to one of a community funding the construction of nine contextually designed roads rather than ten utilitarian designs, opposition groups will allow the decisionmakers to make the quality choice in the context of the bigger picture.

Faced with an imminent public development proposal, the opposition might seek to push construction into the next budgetary cycle so that questions of how may be appropriately answered and funded. If the proponent pleads an emergency, remember that there are few instances where a community will not be well served by ensuring that design and construction proceed only in accordance with its vision. Communities must live with public works projects for many years. If it takes one budget cycle delay to achieve contextual design, so be it.

Allow me to share a number of basic questions designed to enhance the opposition strategy:

1. What is the group agenda? The group's goals and priorities? (We will discuss this topic separately in chapter 5.)
2. What style of approach will the opposition adopt? What approach will most likely achieve its purpose?

3. What is the basis of the group's objections—actual, not merely emotional?

4. Is there hope for compromise or friendly resolution, or will this be a fight that goes into the fourteenth round?

5. What are the likely financial impacts of the proposal? Who are the logical allies of the opposition who might be willing to contribute moral and financial support to its efforts?

6. Are professionals needed to explain the proposal and help prepare the opposition's presentation? If so, how are those professionals to be chosen? Who will pay them?

7. What financial resources are available to the opposition, and what are the likely costs and benefits of a concerted effort?

8. What resources or skills does the opposition have that might be drawn upon?

9. How much time and effort is it going to take to win?

10. How far has the proposal proceeded, and will the opposition have the time to make an informed presentation?

11. What facts have apparently not been considered?

12. Is the proponent or municipal staff stating something as a fact that is merely a point of view? Have the opposition's facts been substantively addressed or considered?

13. What are viable alternative designs/options which might equally advance the needs of the proponent?

14. What is the basic philosophy which underlies the proposal and any alternative designs?

Few opposition groups ask these most basic questions. Generally, group strategy unfolds spontaneously in the public debate. There are two types of such unplanned strategy, *turn up the volume* and *constrained chaos*. Another strategy, *pure political heat*, involves more foresight but doesn't achieve better results. The *full court press* is the only approach that I recommend.

TURN UP THE VOLUME

This approach seems to come naturally to most opposition groups. It is designed to overwhelm the proponent and decisionmakers through participation and the volume of objections. Citizens pack public hearings and deliver impassioned speeches at the highest possible decibel level. Turn up the volume is characterized by invocations of constitutional rights and taxpayer rights, predictions of doom and gloom, and disparagement of others' motives.

There are pluses to this approach. Often participants draw upon a reservoir of common sense. Also, a large turnout at public meetings may, in some cases, help decisionmakers gauge the depth of opposition.

Two relevant examples were reported by the Dubuque, Iowa, *Telegraph Herald*. On February 6, 1996, the *Telegraph Herald* reported on a proposal to rezone a lawn and garden shop to allow it to sell guns near a school. The proposal is typical of that confronted by many cities and towns. After 132 residents petitioned the city council and were joined by the principal of the affected school, the petition was quickly denied. This was a common sense issue and a common sense result that didn't require legions of experts to resolve.

On April 30, 1996, the *Telegraph Herald* reported on another proposal, this one by the Wisconsin and Iowa National Guards, to establish a low-fly zone in a 180-mile area extending from Madison, Wisconsin, to Vinton, Iowa. Such zones enable military pilots to train at altitudes as low as 300 feet. A local farmer researched the effects of low-fly zones on the ground and formed an opposition group of citizens called Citizens United Against Low Level Flights. The group generated attendance of 200 people at one public workshop and obtained the signatures of 3,000 people on a petition opposing the designation. They won. The political reality caused the Guard to withdraw the proposal.

Tuning Out

Turn up the volume isn't always so successful. As you have learned to ignore your children's loud boom box, decisionmakers may learn to tune you out. Furthermore, decisionmakers will have to follow certain legal standards that you will be in no position to question. Or they may have to balance the scales in favor of the collective interest of the community, even if to the detriment of your neighborhood.

The high-volume approach may also be marred by personal attacks, which tend to sour the process for all and which may even discourage opponents from taking part. Personal attacks almost always alienate decisionmakers and result in poor decisions.

CONSTRAINED CHAOS

This is much like turn up the volume but often less effective. Usually it is a variation of the first approach with the added ingredient of a single attorney. Everyone feels that an attorney is necessary, although no one can afford one, so someone in the group enlists the support of her attorney, the one she used in a personal injury or divorce case, for the purpose of making an impassioned speech to the decision-making body. Or the attorney will make long recitations of the municipal code and bald assertions about how standards are not being followed. The attorney receives no professional support because the opposition group cannot afford it.

The dangers of this approach should be obvious to all. Decisionmakers are easily repelled by a battle of the attorneys, especially in the public forum, and when all is said and done they may well turn to the municipal attorney and rely on his or her opinion. Moreover, the attorney's presence removes the presumption of non-representation. Decisionmakers are less likely to make a case for you.

It is wise to remember that all attorneys are not created equal. Some simply lack the skills to succeed in the public forum, even if they are terrific litigators or have reputations as the biggest gorillas in the jungle.

Finally, bringing an attorney to a meeting won't impress anybody. A lawyer's bombastic speech may antagonize people, but it won't scare them. If fear is the object, forget it.

The one real advantage of an attorney is that your objections will be preserved for the public record. This is especially important in jurisdictions where preservation is a condition for maintaining subsequent litigation or administrative appeal.

PURE POLITICAL HEAT

This approach is the most distasteful approach and usually leads to the worst possible decisions. It is amazing how many opponents make public deliberation a test of political wills. I know Sue the commissioner and I have known her all of her life. She just can't vote against me—Wrong, she can and will, especially if you resort to political arm twisting.

Pure political heat is a lazy method of opposition because in theory it is a short cut. No muss, no fuss. But political heat is a path to disaster. If you play this game you legitimize it, meaning that if the proponent or some other group has more political chips, it wins, and you can hardly cry foul.

THE FULL COURT PRESS

This is the approach that I prefer and almost exclusively use. It requires an in-depth examination and public discussion of the facts. In other words, it is a battle of substance that relies on proper preparation, the creation of public awareness, the expectation of accountability, an effective network of communication, and a clear articulation of what is acceptable. What are the alternatives?

By adopting the full court press you signal that you expect intellectual honesty, and you make proponents play in your sandbox, not theirs. This is the proponent's worst nightmare: informed, thoughtful opposition. It will often earn the respect of the proponent, creating an environment which lends itself to the best land planning solutions.

The full court press is not for the lazy. Nor is it for the faint of heart. It requires that you be armed with facts. You must know as much about the proposal as the proponent. You must approach the proponent with quiet intensity and conviction. You must have confidence. The full court press anticipates the proponent's arguments in detail and develops logical responses.

The full court press will appeal to the greatest number of people. People like to be appreciated and part of well orchestrated efforts. For opposition leaders, the full court press, properly designed and executed, offers the greatest hope for participation and success.

Decisionmaking that depends on turn up the volume, constrained chaos, or pure political heat will almost always harm the community. Decisions made on the basis of who is stroking whom at what cocktail party or golf club fail to consider the welfare of all, and, as a result, lack substance.

The remainder of this book is dedicated to explaining the full court press. Please understand that while intense, the strategy is highly adaptable to many different problems, resources, and budgets. Don't be discouraged if you cannot finance the mother of all land use wars. We all must work within our means.

CHAPTER 5

Setting the Agenda

Setting the opposition agenda is the cornerstone of strategic thought. Well defined and broadly understood goals keep all members interested in the effort. Goals, listed in order of priority, are targets against which performance can be measured. And tightly woven agendas make meetings more efficient, respecting the time constraints of each participant, and helping prevent conversational drift.

The random act of government, developer, or neighbor for out-of-context development often unites people previously unknown to each other. Well defined agendas give them something in common.

Citizens are drawn to the opposition through a common concern. It is incumbent on the leaders of the opposition to capitalize on this concern by establishing clearly defined goals. Agendas are starting points. They define goals and possible solutions, effectively asking each opposition member: Is this worth fighting for?

Clearly defined agendas bind members of the opposition. Without the agenda, they are a group of individuals acting individually. If acting individually, they are easy game for the proponent, who will simply divide and conquer.

Agendas come in all shapes and sizes. To develop yours, perhaps it would help to consider two contrasting extremes.

At one extreme is the agenda which I call the *just say no* agenda. The just say no agenda tends to define the object in crystal clear terms: Say no to the development! The group is united in that its mission is clearly understood. Do not let the development proceed in any form. No compromises. No means no.

For certain types of proposals the just say no agenda is very appropriate. For instance, in the example of a proposal to allow commercial jets at the local airport, the decision is black and white. Also in the case of beach hardening proposals: construction either is or is not allowed. If encouraged, the construction may save structures close to the water but sacrifice the beach, a public resource. In environmental questions concerning preservation and conservation, a community will have to adopt a philosophically based result. There are not many intermediate resolutions available. Once gone, resources are lost forever.

The just say no agenda has the advantage of simplicity and of being clearly understood. But it also has disadvantages in certain cases. The major disadvantage is that it often does not lead to a conclusion. As a consequence, the opposition is constantly fighting the same fight. This is especially true where the proposal involves private property rights and new proposed development. The land owner has some right to reasonable use of his property and is going to be back again and again until it is clear what use can be made of it.

Several years ago a group of property owners living adjacent to the Naples, Florida, airport opposed a proposed affordable housing project which was being supported by the City of Naples. The city proposed the annexation of a property in Collier County because it was contiguous to the airport. The city concurrently proposed to rezone the property from county densities of three units per acre to an affordable housing density of from twelve to sixteen units per acre. The adjacent property owners lived in single-family homes on each side of the tract; however, the neighborhood was clearly in transition, with the historical uses under significant economic pressure for redevelopment. It was politically more expedient for the city to locate its required affordable housing next to the airport than within proximity to the central urban area.

Initially, the opposing property owners adopted a just say no agenda. They offered no possibility of compromise. The problem with this approach was that it would have kept an undesirable status quo. The city would not have met its affordable housing requirements. The owner of the proposed development site would not have received a definite answer to the question of what best to do with his property in a transitional neighborhood. Clearly, however, annexing the property for noncontextual development was not a good solution. The just say no agenda was not going to be effective without an alternative proposal that accommodated competing interests.

After months of acrimonious public debate and presentations to the Naples Planning Advisory Board, the Naples City Council, and various regional and county bodies, the issue was resolved. The solution addressed both the city's and county's affordable housing needs. Under the agreement, the concerned municipalities shared credits for affordable housing densities. This eliminated the need for annexation. Furthermore, the property owner was given the opportunity to appear before the county with a request for increased densities limited to affordable housing. (He never did.) This was a logical resolution.

Another disadvantage of just say no is that opponents might actually get what they are asking for. Opposition groups should always pose the question, What happens if the development is not approved? The answer is not always a better development plan. Developers frequently build horribly intrusive developments as a matter of right. Different development is not always better.

There is a property in a commercial center about one mile from my home at the intersection of a major arterial and a collector street. Target, a national chain department store, made a proposal to locate a regional store there. This was met by immediate opposition from the adjacent neighborhood on the grounds of a minor traffic issue (the location of an entry drive) that could have been easily resolved. A Wal-Mart stands on the location today.

The opposite extreme is an agenda of *capitulation.* Capitulation accepts inevitable loss. It is surrender before the opposition even starts. Opponents simply meet with the proponent and accept whatever is offered, confessing that they are unwilling to fight.

Capitulation has the advantage of being quick, final, and efficient. At best, it preserves the record of concern. This may be important when a given project has an impact on a community that was identified by the opposition but not widely understood. When the developer returns to the decisionmakers with a request for municipal funding for a remedy to the problem, you can remind the developer that the initial condition was foreseeable. The developer then bears the expense of the remedy.

Most agendas fall between just say no and capitulation, in the *pragmatic center.* These agendas recognize that development proposals may represent an opportunity for community improvement. Inherently, they are open to compromise.

In defining the agenda, two key questions should be answered.

First, what would the effects of the proposed development be, and to what degree, if any, might these be mitigated? Developments present not only potential problems but also the opportunity to solve existing problems. For example, a planned-unit development adjacent to an existing neighborhood may represent an opportunity to enhance right-of-way landscaping, pedestrian pathways, or recreational areas such as public parks or beaches. In many communities, development may lead to the conservation of environmentally sensitive lands through the voluntary imposition of development restrictions. Often, developers are willing to construct public amenities such as parks, sidewalks, lighting, landscaping, and road improvements that benefit not only their proposed projects but also adjacent neighborhoods. This is also true of development projects proposed by government.

Second, what might the unstated impacts of the proposal be? Often, the most onerous consequences are those that were not addressed or anticipated. On a local level, unforeseen consequences may emanate from a lack of local expertise. Often nearby communities will have dealt with a similar development issue. Yet local officials, sometimes because of financial constraints, hesitate to look beyond the county line for their engineering, planning, and scientific expertise.

Beach hardening proposals are common examples. Beach hardening is the construction of concrete structures to protect eroding beaches. At a time when most states recognize the dramatic loss of sandy beach, and thus public access, caused by the construction of beach hardening devices, the State of Florida has ceded control of emergency permitting of these devices to local governments. Local decisions permitting the construction of groins, segmented breakwaters, rock revetments, and sea walls to shore up a beach may be sanctioned by local coastal engineers who are committed to a philosophy of beach hardening even though many respected coastal geologists have maintained that the aggregate effect of hardening is to eliminate sandy beach. Rarely do coastal communities rely on the latest science; the views of the local engineer with a vested interest in designing such devices tend to hold sway. These communities suffer with the results of beach hardening, the loss of sandy beaches, because they lack the will or foresight to consider non-local points of view.

Once you've answered these questions, it is time to establish priorities. Draft a menu of alternative results or improvements that would make a given development work. Then classify their relative importance. You might want to do so in this way:

> *Must have.* What objectives must the opposition accomplish under any circumstances? These objectives cannot and will not be compromised even though the consequence may be the expenditure of time and money in public hearings and litigation.
>
> *Should have.* What objectives are worth fighting for and will clearly enhance the quality of the development? These will only be compromised in the face of certain loss.
>
> *Great to have.* These objectives will enhance the development choice but might be accomplished with or without it. If the development will serve as a means of accomplishing them, then these objectives should be pursued.
>
> *Don't need, but serve as a bonus.* These objectives will make the development better but cannot be legally imposed, or in the case of the government proponent, are not anticipated or funded as future improvements. These objectives are frequently the opposition's negotiating tool.

This scheme of classification identifies not only your objectives, but also what sort of effort you are willing to make to achieve each one.

Is the objective to avoid the development proposal completely, or are there circumstances under which it could work? Usually, the opposition requires professional advice to formulate an answer to this question. Development often creates planning opportunities. The strategic challenge for opponents is to know what to ask for.

Too many opposition groups don't know what to ask for because they aren't versed in design and planning. This is where professionals can make a big difference. Planners, engineers, architects, scientists, and others will help opposition groups understand what can and should be accomplished in the context of a given proposal.

Opposition groups might also consult the resources of national organizations involved in planning, science, and governmental decision making. I have listed and provided address information (including web addresses) for a number of these organizations in appendix A.

In land use battles, resolutions tend to gravitate towards a pragmatic center, the proverbial splitting of the difference. Do not, in a search for pragmatism, find the mediocre resolution. In defining an agenda and establishing priorities, you are seizing the opportunity to raise community standards. Therefore, shoot high. Establish lofty goals. Proponents always do. They constantly ask for more than they expect to receive, leaving themselves room for compromise. Ask for everything that would make the proposal community friendly.

What must you have? What should you have? What would it be great to have? What would serve as a bonus?

CHAPTER 6

Preliminary Fact-Finding

B efore an agenda is fully established and any professionals are retained, opponents should go on a fact-finding mission. They should try to gather as much information as possible about the proposal, its history, and its potential effects. And they must make sure that no information is provided to the media that is not factual and verified.

Early and detailed fact-finding is critical for several reasons.

First, opponents must make certain that they are on solid ground. Credibility once lost is difficult to regain, among allies and decisionmakers alike. It is remarkable how much misinformation can be disseminated early in the public life of a development proposal. The local newspaper or radio may publicize initial positions of opponents that are patently false.

Media misinformation is often not intentional. Reporters may be dispatched to unfamiliar parts of the community and asked to report on development proposals that have a long and complicated history. Then they are given a sixty-second sound bite or five hundred words to explain the proposal, the proponent's position, and opposition questions.

The danger for opponents is this: Relying on misinformation will not instill confidence in others who may have legitimate questions of their own. Further, when the misinformation is brought to light, which is inevitable, proponents will characterize your opposition as fully developed, claiming that all legitimate questions have been answered and that there really wasn't anything to worry about after all. The proponents will win the war for the public heart and soul before the first battle is fought. There may still be valid questions that haven't been brought to light, but now they never will be. The public has made up its mind.

Second, early and detailed fact-finding helps develop a cohesive agenda and strategy.

In the early stages of opposition, a tremendous amount of time and energy is often spent speculating about the proponent's intentions. Time and energy will be sorely needed later on, before and during public hearings. If they are expended before the plane leaves the runway, the opposition will never get off the ground. Solid fact-finding, not speculation, is the way to fuel your effort.

Third, being correctly informed early will send a message to the proponent that the opposition is credible, perhaps even formidable. The proponent's perception of your preparedness will influence what he asks for, what may be conceded, and what is subject to negotiation. Often these judgments are formed early on, when development applications are being considered by the public.

Finally, fact-finding is crucial to limiting costs and conserving financial resources. It is exponentially more cost-effective to approach your counsel for advice with a clear and complete story in the first consultation. If you leave it up to a professional to scrounge around for information, you may be paying two hundred dollars per hour.

So what information is helpful, and how do you find it? You want to know the following:

1. Who are the individuals pushing the development proposal, and what are their positions and backgrounds ?
2. What is the exact nature of the proposal? If it is for construc-

tion, what is the density or how many units are proposed, and over what period will they be built? Is there a proposed site plan? How detailed is it?

3. Have permit applications been filed or reviewed, and with which local, state, and federal agencies? When were the applications filed? What is the process for review and approval? What are the names, positions, and addresses of those responsible for review of applications?

4. What documents or correspondence might be available pertaining to permits or the development application? Are there photographs or maps of the property subject to the proposal? A picture often is worth a thousand words.

5. What documents might regulate the development? For instance, is there a relevant planned-unit ordinance? Are there deed restrictions described in homeowner documentation? What city or county ordinances apply? What state statutes apply? Are minutes or resolutions from previous public hearings available?

6. What are the names, positions, and addresses of the professionals retained by the proponent, and what are their special talents?

7. Does the property under consideration have any development or permitting history?

8. What is the time line for the development?

9. Apart from development approvals, what are the proponent's actual plans, and what hurdles might the proponent have to overcome other than government approvals? For example, permitted developments are often able to obtain financing only if a certain percentage of the property is pre-leased (in the case of commercial development), or pre-sold (in the case of residential). Does the proponent have to acquire any property which it either doesn't own or doesn't have under contract?

The above list is not all inclusive, but it will give you an idea of the sorts of questions you should be seeking answers to. If the list seems formidable, don't be alarmed. This kind of information is surprisingly easy to assemble. Start with a public records act request. Virtually every state has an act allowing citizens access to public records merely by letter of request. Depending on the state, letters submitted to local planning departments or state agencies must be answered within a defined period, usually not exceeding thirty days. The most complete method is to ask for copies of all documents relating to a certain project or proposal, including correspondence, application materials, staff notes or memoranda, and notes of meetings with the developer or its representatives.

Most states publish sunshine manuals that describe the public records statute and how to make a formal request. These can often be obtained from the attorney general's office or the local clerk. Florida's sunshine manual has been posted on the Internet.

Much of the same information can be had directly from the local planning board or state agency simply by asking the staff person responsible for review for access to the files. A trip to the local development services office or planning agency can yield a tremendous amount of information. Do both informal and formal information gathering, so that if a staff person neglects to provide documentation that may be critical, you can always later point to the formal request as a procedural mistake. In other words, you followed the rules—the staff didn't. This may be grounds for rehearing on appeal of a development approval.

In a recent case, I discovered a memorandum in a staff file written by a proponent's attorney in which he strongly suggested how a staff report to the county commission should be rewritten. Imagine the likely surprise of the county commissioners if they should learn that a proponent had written part of their staff report!

Another formal method of fact-finding is a pre-emptive letter requesting that the agency provide *all* future information pertaining to a certain proposal. This method is especially effective if a neighborhood, community organization, or individual is aware of a proposed development early in the permitting process. In addition to asking for information, the letter should request direct notice of any and all future public hearings. Or, if hearings are not planned, the letter could request that one be held.

Such letters can have an impact. They tend to create accountability in the permitting process. The reviewer knows that someone besides the proponent is watching, and that his or her actions will be scrutinized at some later date. Knowing that someone took the time to write the letter or request, the reviewer may look at the proposal more critically.

Then there is the federal Freedom of Information Act. Backed by this legislation, a citizen can unearth a wealth of information for projects requiring federal permits or for which exemptions from federal jurisdiction have been requested. There are many other federal statutes and regulations that allow citizens to gather specific information. The Army Corps of Engineers, Environmental Protection Agency, and Interior Department all have such regulations.

EXEMPTIONS

Developers or government proponents often go to decisionmakers, or their staff, and ask to be exempted from full administrative reviews of their proposal because of its relatively small size or nature. The importance of these determinations for opponents is that they may not have a forum for objection to these proposals in a formal hearing process.

Another way to collect information is simply by talking with municipal, state, or federal staff. They work for you and are trained to respond to public requests. Initial meetings with the proponents themselves may bring some answers—before expensive attorneys are hired.

In certain instances, you might question local reporters as to what the proponents are telling them in the hopes of publication. Reporters have an interest in creating a level playing field and tend to want to share information unless they're afraid of violating a privilege. If you don't approach reporters, at least make a point of clipping any articles they write. And don't forget to consult neighbors and local historians. They can be a great aid, especially in supplying a historical perspective on a property subject to development.

Once your information is assembled, organize it chronologically, so that it tells a story. This will help members of the opposition to absorb the facts and more readily identify strengths and weaknesses in their position.

Remember, knowledge is the currency of the full court press. So build the foundation for opposition success through early, complete, and thorough preparation.

CHAPTER 7

Professional Consultants
Using and Choosing Them

*C*axambas Pass, Marco Island, Florida, has served as an unimpeded means of navigation for pleasure boaters and fishermen since the advent of historical records. In the 1960s the federal government built a missile tracking station on the northernmost shore of the inlet and sea-walled the island end abutting the pass. Consequently the pass has not required dredging for decades, an unusual condition for passes on the west coast of Florida. The natural channel, nine feet deep at mean low tide, provides the sole water access for over two thousand homes and a county boat-launching facility.

Around 1990 a developer purchased the abandoned missile tracking station for development of high-rise luxury condominiums and, together with a beach renourishment constituency, supported an earlier proposal to install segmented breakwaters offshore. The idea behind the proposal was that the breakwaters would anchor the south end of the Marco Island beach renourishment project as well as reduce erosion in front of the developer's site. Everyone, including advocates of the proposal, agreed that the breakwater installation would probably fill in the natural channel. That was the intention. As a result, however, an alternative channel would have to be dredged, an uncertain and expensive process.

Advocates for the proposal were well organized. They advanced their case with the help of a former Army Corps engineer during the summer of 1995, when two-thirds of the island's population were gone. The advisory committee showed the county board that there were unspent funds available from a special taxing district, funds that had no other apparent purpose. Public money with nowhere to go is usually a prescription for land use disaster. The advocates lobbied several political leaders, saying they had broad support on the island and bolstering their position with the claim that emergency conditions existed: sand placed in front of the sea wall during a previous beach renourishment project had eroded faster than predicted.

Several meetings of an island beach renourishment advisory board were held during the summer of 1995 to discuss the proposal. A few boaters who happened to be around attended the meetings, where they were promptly dismissed as unruly and purely driven by self-interest. The proposal was pushed forward to the county commission for funding during August, when many citizens were away on vacation. An emergency environment was created by the proponents; they were going to save money by taking an unexpectedly low bid of $550,000. Further, they claimed that installation would have to begin in October 1995 so as not to affect turtle nesting later in the year.

This threw the boaters into a panic. They wanted a lawsuit to stop the proposal dead in its tracks. They consulted with an attorney at a major local firm who recognized the need for outside expertise. He referred the opponents to an out-of- town firm that promptly asked for a large retainer. The opponents balked. The county commission meeting at which funding was to be considered was one week away and they had no expert advice. Other attorneys with whom they consulted played hot potato, passing the problem on to someone else because they weren't willing to get involved without some form of professional engineering support. The opponents attended the meeting without representation and were dismissed by the county commission, which relied on the advice of its coastal engineer and the beach renourishment advisory board to fund the proposed contract and proceed with the project.

The project, despite its emergency status, was not initiated as quickly as planned. This gave the opponents a window in which they arranged for review of the proposal by Dr. Orrin H. Pilkey, one of the most respected coastal geologists in the country. Dr. Pilkey, after scrutinizing the plans and doing an aerial site inspection, determined that not only would the installation probably not protect the beach, it might actually aggravate erosion in the renourished area. His findings were widely reported at a town hall meeting called by the opponents and in the local press. The proponents of the project, most of whom did not have time to attend the meeting, quickly dismissed Dr. Pilkey as biased.

The opponents finally initiated an administrative action challenging the installation of the breakwaters. Their grounds? Harm to navigation and the alleged failure of the proponents to follow procedure. Meanwhile, however, sixty tons of boulders have been placed in the channel. Why did this result occur?

The boaters' position is a strong one for two reasons. First, segmented breakwaters are an experimental coastal engineering device that have a history of failure. Second, the decision to spend hundreds of thousands of public dollars on an uncertain result in an attempt to create a beach primarily for a future condominium complex, while incurring the expense of regular dredging at several hundred thousand dollars a pop, defies logic. So why didn't the boaters succeed right off the bat?

HIRING CONSULTANTS

I use this example because the boaters were forced into a position of fighting the proposal without the benefit of complete professional representation. They were placed on a short fuse with virtually no margin for error in a field, coastal construction, where there is a limited amount of expertise. They were forced into the approaches of turn up the volume and constrained chaos, and then into litigation, without the benefit of having their side of the story properly explained in the public forum.

Even when opponents have the choice of using professional representation early, their natural inclination is to adopt the approaches of turn up the volume or constrained chaos. Almost all citizens expect their government to protect them and to regulate in a way that fosters compatible land uses.

Rarely does an opposition group enlist professionals early on. The most pressing reason is usually financial constraints, real or perceived. People don't readily reach into their pockets unless they are absolutely convinced that they have to. Opponents pay taxes, which are supposed to pay for protecting their quality of life. When that protection breaks down, paying for professional representation seems like the equivalent of double paying. You pay taxes for protection. Then you pay independent professionals to protect you from your protectors.

In fact, everyone is a taxpayer, even a development corporation, and all have the right to petition and avail themselves of government processes. Even when the situation is viewed in this light, however, opponents are never building or adding to their quality of life, only protecting the status quo. In financial planning terms, they are preserving their assets.

More often, opponents experience the baptism of a hearing or two before confronting the stark reality that the proponent's professionals and their advance work just might prevail. This revelation commonly comes within a week or two of the final hearing. Then opponents have to scramble around for professionals who are willing to step in front of a speeding locomotive—for free, or something close to it—in the hopes that the proponent's train can be derailed.

By bringing professionals in at the ninth hour, after a proposed development has been fully explored at an administrative or planning board level, opponents may seriously jeopardize their position, foregoing the best legal or other means to success.

How often do citizens appear at the final land use hearing, often not represented, in a process that may have spanned several months or years, and claim that the development proposals haven't been subject to enough public discussion, then ask for further delay? Usually not a winning argument. Because the proponent is close to success they elect to show up and raise an issue that could have been raised at the first hearing. The law is not sympathetic to such naïveté about procedure, which as most commissioners know is often plain apathy.

The irony of not hiring professionals early on for lack of funds is that retaining them at the end of the public hearing stage tends to be far more costly. This is true for several reasons.

First, it is difficult if not impossible to educate professionals at the tail end of a public hearing process.

Second, it is much easier for professionals to help opponents prevail in the earlier stages of opposition. Many statutes allow administrative hearings to be requested at both federal and state levels. Virtually all statutes require that opponents receive all requested documents and notices of all public hearings for the price of postage. If someone makes these requests on your behalf and registers your interest, you greatly diminish the cost of subsequent fact gathering.

Third, decisionmakers and staff won't intractably favor the proponent if they sense opposition early in the permitting and zoning processes. In the absence of visible opposition, they will do as much to accommodate the proponent as they would a constituent.

Fourth, early involvement of professionals sends a message to proponents that you are committed in your opposition. This discourages them from proceeding without addressing your concerns, that is, before they have gone hard with the plans. This is an important point in terms of both time and money, for proponents spend an increasing amount of money drafting plans and committing to those plans as permitting and review proceed. Over time, proponents' positions become more and more inflexible.

Finally, professionals can help opposition groups identify weaknesses in development proposals, and potential solutions, early on. For example, in conflicts between neighbors involving obstruction of view, architects may be able to come up with design solutions that would minimize the problem. In cases of road design, engineers, landscape architects, and planners may together be able to identify the opportunity and cost for competing designs that would beautify the neighborhood while making it safer.

And don't forget—having professional backing at public hearings helps level the playing field. Your public complaints will be perceived as whining if they lack a well-developed factual and legal basis. Professionals make proponents accountable. Professionals make opponents credible.

As opponents, you cannot ignore the apparent. Ours is a society of rule by law. Often the laws are fairly sophisticated. The proponents of development know the rules. They hire professionals capable of delivering them to the promised land. Opponents must seek a similar advantage and similar understanding.

CHOOSING CONSULTANTS

One Christmas when I was in high school, my dad, tired of having my brothers and me expropriate his tools, gave tool boxes to all us. On the top of each box was an inscription: Each tool has a place, each tool in its place, use the right tool for the right job. And so it is in selecting land use professionals as consultants—you must find the right people for the right job.

Most development opponents lack the experience to select and manage professionals. All too often, the opponents end up at the mercy of the people they happen upon by chance.

What sort of professional consultants will you need? How will you select them? (Assume for now that money is not an obstacle.) The first step in answering these questions is to look to the proponents. Whom have they hired?

In comparatively minor cases, the proponent's team may be small. In neighbor versus neighbor cases, for instance, it could be limited to an architect, contractor, and attorney. In more involved projects such as residential golf course developments, the proponent's team is likely to be larger and more specialized, perhaps including planners, civil, transportation, utilities, and environmental engineers, surveyors, lawyers, architects, appraisers, and golf course designers.

In either case, the proponent's team is a collection of consultants each with a defined role. They communicate well. And they are expected to cooperate for the purpose of achieving the proponent's well defined goals.

Understanding the needs of proponents in establishing their team enables opponents to grasp their own needs. If, for instance, a developer proposes a location for a commercial mall because of assumptions about population growth and traffic patterns, he has used a site planner, a transportation planner, and a transportation engineer. He has probably also used a commercial feasibility expert to justify the economic need for such a development. If opponents expect to understand and challenge all of these assumptions, they will need consultants from the same disciplines. Both sides will undoubtedly have attorneys as well.

But scrutinizing the proponent's choices is not always sufficient. Are there disciplines that the proponent has not considered but that may be important to a full understanding of the effects of a development?

Often this is so. For example, developers may engineer and propose projects without considering environmental impacts. In that case, opponents would be wise to consider retaining scientists or environmental consultants who can articulate any unexpected consequences when communicating with the proponent and with decisionmakers and their staff.

Or the proponent may hire specialized consultants when consultants with broader training might be more suitable. Shore communities, for example, might use coastal engineers to advise them on beach hardening such as groins, break walls, and revetments, devices designed for coastal protection. Coastal geologists, who understand how such devices affect long stretches of shoreline in specific cases, may be better equipped to identify their long-term effects.

Feasibility

Feasibility refers to the economic viability of given land uses. Developers generally do not want this type of financial information to be made public. However, the question of feasibility is often brought into play when the developer claims that he cannot afford to build with less residential density, less commercial square footage, or higher-quality public amenities. The question of the economic feasibility of a proposed use is always legitimate.

Or the proponent may make broad, unsupported statements, leaving the door open for the opposition. This often occurs in financial assumptions and representations. For instance, a developer stands before a municipal body claiming to need a certain density, commercial square footage, or site plan. Are his financial figures accurate? And how do they compare to the potential financial disadvantages of the development or an alternative design? Certified appraisers experienced in development, particularly feasibility, can be effective consultants for opponents. They might also provide insight into what can be achieved in discussions aimed at a friendly resolution.

In considering which consultants to hire, opponents should, of course, take a look at their goals.

If, for instance, a school district proposes a school on a busy arterial road, people opposed to its location might define their "must have" objective as a traffic signal. They might define their "should have" objective as siting the school away from the arterial. In either case, they will need the help of both a traffic consultant and an attorney. It may be that a planner or engineer would also prove useful. The planner or engineer might be able to help with lesser objectives, such as lighting, landscaping, or site planning for the safe pick-up of students.

Once you have decided what types of consultants to hire, you must consider the individuals themselves. All land use consultants are not created equal. Their effectiveness depends on the sort of development at issue, their experience, their ability to relate to the opponents as clients, and the identity of other professional consultants. Here are some questions to consider in building your professional team:

Is the consultant experienced in the type of land use matter at issue? Remember, the most talented consultants often limit their representation to the development community, where the financial reward is greatest. Consultants also receive the clearest direction and face fewer organizational challenges working for the proponent. Few consultants can make a living in the desert of community representation.

Has the consultant had at least some experience in developer or government representation? It is difficult for a consultant to understand development economics or to anticipate the proponent's arguments unless he or she has been there.

What is the consultant's public persona? You should hire someone with presence, confidence, and understanding, and not simply because of a reputation as the biggest gorilla on the block. Bombastic egos generally don't make it far in public chambers.

Does the consultant have experience in the public forum? Consultants should not be intimidated by large crowds and media that turn out at public hearings on controversial issues. Nor should they be intimidated by the precise and demanding questions of decisionmakers. Public hearings are not a place for shrinking violets.

Is the consultant able to keep his composure in emotional situations, which is what land use matters tend to be? Your representative must be thinking and orchestrating clearly.

Can the consultant identify with your cause? Will she be able to relate to the proponent and decisionmakers? Stuffed shirts and practical, hardworking opponents may not mix.

Is the consultant willing to spend the time with you? If he does not thoroughly understand your position, he won't be able to explain it to a decisionmaker. Will he personally take the time to explain all conclusions relevant to your decisions? Will the consultant attend opposition group meetings when necessary?

Is the consultant a team player? Can she work with other professionals and members of the opposition, or does her ego demand that she be in the limelight?

Will the consultant always recognize that your interests come first?

Has the consultant participated in community groups, preferably neighborhood associations? This experience will have given him insight into the unique challenges associated with communication and decisionmaking in community groups.

Will the consultant provide honest opinions, not necessarily those you want to hear? If she guarantees success, be cautious.

Is the consultant frank regarding fee arrangements? Willing to put all agreements in writing?

Does your professional have credibility with the county commission, city council, or state or federal hearing officer? The land use case should be won on the facts, not on the flamboyance or emotional rhetoric of the consultant.

Is the professional given to merely applying standards and written regulations? Or does the professional understand the philosophies and science which underlie the regulations and laws which will govern the development proposal?

If possible, take the time to solicit recommendations, to interview candidates, and to ask them for written resumes and proposals. Ask consultants how they would analyze the development proposal and how they might help identify both problems and solutions.

Having consultants is never enough. Having the best consultants may mean the difference between success and failure. It is up to you to find the right tool for the job.

CHAPTER 8

Financing
the Opposition

M*oney* is the greatest challenge facing opponents of inappropriate development. Will the opposition be able to raise the funds it needs to make a case for the best development choice? Opponents may have great legal arguments, citizen involvement, and public support for their position, but the fact remains that framing and presenting arguments in a public forum take money.

The opposition group that lacks professional representation will almost always be a step behind the proponent. It will not be properly equipped to evaluate the development proposal; to establish objectives in an informed way; to establish effective dialogue with the proponent; and most importantly, to develop the factual and legal arguments that are a must in denying or modifying the proposal.

Money is one area where the proponent clearly has the edge. He is usually out to make a profit, and money expended in the application process is an investment. In a sense, even the government proponent views such expenditure as an investment, for it has a bearing on the growth and health of the community. Opponents' motivations are quite different: preserving quality of life and protecting the value of existing assets. Opponents rarely view dollars spent as an investment.

Proponents also have the advantage of timing. They know, when they first introduce their proposal, the approximate cost that might be associated with the application process and where the money will come from. They have a firm understanding of their risks and potential rewards. Opponents, on the other hand, must constantly assess and reassess their goals, as well as their risks and potential rewards, and they must make these judgments relatively quickly.

As opponents, how do you overcome these obstacles? The answer is that you must approach the financing of your effort as you would a business decision—strategically. Allow me to share what I call the five steps of strategic financial planning:

1. Establish a range of costs for achieving each of your goals.

What are your goals and what will it cost to obtain each? Cost projections are a shot in the dark, because there is much that you just don't know. For instance, is it possible that you will reach a friendly resolution with the proponent at an early stage? Or will you be fighting to the death for must have priorities?

Incremental cost analysis is often helpful. You might consider breaking pre-litigation opposition into phases. Then you can ask how much will be spent for segment one, for segment two, and so forth. Stages might be described as progressing in the following way:

a. Preliminary fact finding and legal research;

b. Negotiation with agency staff;

c. Negotiation with the proponent;

d. Preparation and research before a planning council, board, or local hearing officer; and

e. Appearance in hearings before the city council, town board, or county commission.

What is the likely financial cost attached to each set of goals at each stage? Ask consultants to describe the scope of work they believe each stage will entail. Then ask for fee proposals. These should be put in writing as a line item budget that all members of the opposition review and agree to.

2. Choose a target set of goals and costs.

Now comes the hard step: choosing. Knowing the costs involved, you must decide whether to limit yourself to "must have" goals, or whether you can also strike for the "should have" and "nice to have" ones. Are you and your fellow opponents willing to devote the financial resources necessary to credible advocacy of your goals? Or are you going to tackle them with less than the full financial resources, lessening your chances of success? The second step is a judgment call. You have the best information available. What is your choice?

3. Establish organizational credibility.

Is your organization capable of mounting an effective challenge? This is a question that people will ask themselves before they make any financial commitment to your challenge. Often the question is not asked expressly. Potential backers may make their own judgments based on what they perceive. They'll look for capable and informed leadership, well defined goals, and the means by which these goals are to be reached.

Organization here could be an existing civic group, a neighborhood association, or an ad hoc group of individual opponents. In each case the question of capability will be foremost in members' minds before they buy into the opposition effort through financial contribution.

4. Establish administrative credibility.

This step is often overlooked, particularly in ad hoc organizations. Potential backers must be convinced of the opposition's capability to administer money before they will devote money to the cause. It's like citizens voting for new taxes— unless they understand how a proposed tax is to be spent, they will not vote for the tax proposal.

Certain questions must be answered if the opposition hopes to attract citizens willing to help finance the effort:

Who specifically is going to be responsible for seeing that consultants complete tasks within budget, and who will review professionals' proposals, contracts, and billings?

Who is going to be responsible for making decisions of economic consequence?

Who will sign checks to pay for the opposition effort? (More than one signature should be required.)

In existing organizations such as civic groups or neighborhood associations, many of these questions will already have been answered. Most such organizations have articles and bylaws to define roles and delegate authority, and a board of directors who collectively make decisions.

In the absence of a predefined structure, ad hoc groups often grapple with issues of accountability. Citizens may try to pass the hat, giving the largest financial contributors verbal authorization to make all strategic decisions. This approach only works in the rarest of cases. Citizens generally want to know that they have control of how their money is spent, or at least a say in decisions.

Ad hoc opposition groups should consider establishing a community trust for the limited purpose of providing structure for financial and strategic decision-making. Trustees are given the authority to oversee professionals, decide strategy, and pay bills. They also decide how residual funds are to be disbursed in the event that the purpose of the trust has been served. For instance, the trust may return money to individual contributors, or give it to a civic or neighborhood organization for a specific purpose.

Administrative accountability is one way of instilling confidence in the opposition among people considering whether to join it and help fund it.

5. Establish a source of funds and determine how they will be used.

This is where the proverbial rubber hits the road. Who is going to pay? In many cases there is a short list of probable parties. In the case of issues which threaten a whole community or neighborhood, established citizen organizations are the pockets of immediate resort. If they do not have the funds, at least they have the mechanisms to raise them.

In cases of neighbor versus neighbor, often the only funding available is from a neighbor or group of neighbors acting together. The great irony in these cases is that the financial burden often falls on one neighbor, but the benefits flow to the entire neighborhood or community.

Neighbors who are most affected by another neighbor's noncontextual development are the ones who end up fighting and financing the battle. However, the condition that invites the noncontextual proposal may be common to the entire neighborhood. For example, development standards and zoning regulations may not exist or else be ambiguous. Sometimes proposals are legal but would be so much out of context that they come as a shock to the neighborhood. The neighbor who is the potential victim bears the full financial weight of developing precedent for the entire neighborhood. If that neighbor doesn't pay no one will.

If an individual or the members of a community association believe strongly enough in their opposition to a noncontextual proposal, they will vote with their wallets. If not, they won't. So when the question arises of who is going to pay what, when, and how, potential contributors must not only have confidence in the opposition's goals, structure, and administrative capability—they must also believe that they have an economic or quality of life stake in the outcome. Otherwise the checkbook won't leave the pocket.

Opening citizen's eyes to the disadvantages of a particular development is in and of itself a challenge. It is a process of education that must be built on sound reasoning, not conjecture. This raises an interesting question. Often the opposition's coffers are fattened by a party that is a competitor of the proponent. Should the opposition take their money? If so, does it harm their credibility?

An example reported by the *Wall Street Journal* (June 7, 1996) regards contributions to the opponents of an application to allow reopening of the Sunshine Canyon Valley landfill near Los Angeles. The proposal was made by owners of the site. A competing landfill company apparently paid for a study of the possible effect of an earthquake on the proposed site and contributed it to the opposition effort. Several of the decisionmakers questioned the scientific value of the competing study.

Does the contribution by the competing landfill company cast doubt on the value of the study? Is the study paid for by the competitor any less credible than that prepared by the consultants for the applicant? Or should both studies be examined on their merits regardless of who paid for them? Answers to such questions are subjective. My own answer would be to raise another question: If you are in the lion pit about to become dinner, are you going to ask who threw you a sword?

As opponents, the question inherent in step 5 is: Can you win the vote? Will you be able to educate enough citizens and civic groups to mount a credible challenge backed by sound professional advice?

Financing any voluntary effort is difficult at best. But like it or not, funding is a necessary evil of development opposition.

CHAPTER 9

Launching the Challenge

O nce the strategic background questions have been answered, it is time to launch the challenge. The keys to implementing your plan are, first, getting off to a quick start; second, recognizing time constraints; and third, knowing and protecting your argument.

A QUICK START

The most common mistake is to be slow in responding. Drip, drip, drip, you are cooked! Opposition groups, limited in resources, tend to be graduated in their response as the effort of objection gets under way. No resources, time, or funds are committed without a clearly demonstrated need. The irony is that in the long run, this virtually guarantees a maximum expenditure of resources and the longest possible confrontation. Why?

A slow start sends ambiguous signals to the proponent, municipal or agency staff, and decisionmakers. They have no feeling for the depth of your opposition and how far you are willing to go. They allow for possibilities of compromise that in your mind probably don't exist.

Moreover, graduated response to the proposal draws out public debate. Time is money. Protracted debates cost more.

A slow start also poses the danger of false starts which can be deadly. Your concerns have been answered. No they haven't. Yes they have. It is difficult to rally the troops again and again and again. Neither your opposition members nor your professionals will withstand the yo-yo effect for long.

So, as opponents, commit to a quick start.

THE CONSTRAINTS OF TIME

Time defines the course of land use struggles. How much time do you have to prepare for hearings? Will the passage of time alleviate the harmful impacts of a development or present solutions? If approved, will a project be constructed sooner or later?

For the proponent, time is money. Therefore, his objective is usually to move the proposal forward. Rarely does he want to delay a decision for the sake of pending changes in technology, science, or community dynamics, which might make for a more informed decision. The proponent believes that he has a right to proceed on the basis of present conditions. Frequently, however, the proponent is helped in the long term by changing circumstances.

In contrast, the objective of the opposition is usually to delay the choice in order to more fully develop the opposition stance, or to await developments that might cast the choice in a different light. Often opposition groups adopt a strategy of delay not knowing what the next strategic move might be, just hoping that the proponent will fade away like a bad dream. Opponents might also be pinning their hope on a different political environment, one more favorable for their position. Delay, especially when it is not used to enhance the strength of the opposition, and when the proponent is well funded and committed, is often a losing strategy.

When developing strategy, you should carefully assess how much time there is and how you will use that time. Time commonly dictates strategy. You will clearly be in a different position if the proponent has to spend months or years processing applications as opposed to days or weeks.

Know your key dates. When are submittals to be made? When are hearings scheduled? When are agenda packages mailed to the decisionmakers? Plan to meet those dates. Be precise.

Whatever else happens, don't wait until the last approval to launch your effort. The more approvals the proponent obtains, the greater the presumption of acceptance. In fact, one typical strategy of proponents is to obtain the easy permits first. Then they appear at hearings claiming that there has already been a substantial review of the project.

Time spent in preparation is a precious commodity. Use it to your advantage. Put yourself in a position to win. If you believe that a particular proposal is a poor one and endangers your quality of life, then act on that conviction.

Many citizens studiously avoid the public eye even when they would be the most directly affected by poor development. If there is the slightest possibility that a graduated response might work, they want to believe that it is possible to resolve issues without major conflict. Once again, the failure to act with conviction now may cause them to become more deeply involved later. Developing well prepared positions early on creates the best environment for a resolution.

KNOW AND PROTECT YOUR ARGUMENT

Finally, know and protect your argument. The first step is to go on record as soon as possible by sending a notice letter with the opposition's concerns to elected representatives, the city or county manager, and the municipal or agency staff. Remember, this letter is a notice letter, not a position letter. Its purpose is to identify yourself as a concerned party and to indicate that you have an interest in the development proposal. The notice letter may state broad concerns but should not try to make the case. It may ask questions. It may ask for information. It should ask for copies of staff reports and notice of hearing dates.

There is good reason for *not* stating your position at this stage. Presumably your fact-finding mission is ongoing. If you advance your position without all the facts, it will make you look arbitrary. You were going to object regardless of the facts.

Moreover, as background information accumulates, you will learn much, perhaps finding grounds for even stronger objections than before. If you send a position letter without a thorough grasp of all possible bases for challenge, you run the risk of undermining any later objections. The proponent's strategy will be to meet your initial objections and snuff out any later ones.

If you do feel compelled to state your full position in the first letter, at least mention that you are still researching the proposal and that you reserve the right to add objections at a later date.

CONDITIONAL USES AND VARIANCES

Conditional uses and variances are two types of petitions common to many zoning codes. Conditional uses are sometimes referred to as provisional uses.

Conditional uses are uses which are allowed in zoning districts only after public hearing. They might be appropriate uses in some but not all locations within a district. A church in a residential district is a common example of a conditional use.

A variance is generally a use or a feature of a building normally disallowed by regulations for the zoning district, but for which a property owner requests approval for reasons of undue hardship. Variance petitions almost always require public hearings and approval of the governing body. By law, they are rarely allowed.

Next you must become completely informed and as soon as possible. Preliminary fact-finding steps were suggested in chapter 7. Digest and organize the information. Understand the proposal. Look for resources to understand precedents. Then refine your objections. Part of fact-finding is to become familiar with land use law. It establishes the parameters of your opposition. Understand the rules, or be guided by one who does.

The specific type of approval needed by the proponent will dictate your approach. Approvals carry different legal requirements and allow decisionmakers varying levels of discretion. Conditional use, variance, rezonings, and determinations of comprehensive plan consistency all have different criteria and standards which decisionmakers must follow.

In conditional use matters, the decisionmakers will have comparatively little discretion if criteria in the local ordinance are met. In variance applications, rezonings, and determinations of comprehensive plan consistency, decisionmakers will have more discretion to approve or deny given petitions.

The same is true for federal and state processes that rely on statutes and agency rules. All state and federal agencies have a responsibility to follow these statutes and rules. And they have a fair, though not unlimited, amount of discretion. In contrast, publicly initiated projects usually provide decisionmakers with almost absolute discretion, their decisions being policy determinations that balance competing needs.

Often obscure theories win. Perhaps you will recall the case of the Tellico Dam, which found its way through the courts in the late 1970s and early 1980s. The Tellico Dam was a multi-million-dollar public works project advanced by the Tennessee Valley Authority designed to provide power to rural Tennessee and neighboring states. One small problem: the proponents did not realize or account for the fact that if constructed the dam might destroy the habitat of the snail darter, a two-inch-long fish on the Endangered Species List.

Zygmunt J. B. Plater, then a professor at the University of Tennessee Law School, recognized the issue and represented local residents opposed to the dam. The case went all the way to the Supreme Court, where they prevailed. The construction was forestalled.

It would help if you asked what procedural requirements the proponent has to fulfill. Make sure that he does, and that you seize any procedural opportunity to encourage full and fair public discussion of the proposal.

A note: It has recently become fashionable to ridicule those who use all available legal tools, substantive and procedural, to object to a development proposal, the case of the Tellico Dam being a good example. Opponents are viewed as obstructionists for availing themselves of arguments that don't reflect their real objections. Even some environmentalists question the purity of intentions in such a situation.

Let it be remembered, however, that the public is almost always best served by complete public discussion of development proposals. If there is a law protecting the spotted owl, the green sea turtle, the manatee, or another of the thousands of species of plants and animals that disappear from the earth each year, then the identity of their advocate is of little consequence. The point is that we as a society have concluded that the public interest is best served by protecting endangered creatures. That is why the Endangered Species Act exists. Our laws aren't designed to benefit individual or special interests, though individual and special interests are often served. In theory, our laws are adopted for the benefit of all of society.

Furthermore, since local laws often don't account for the macro impacts of helter-skelter development, opposition groups confronted by poor development must use whatever legal means are available until local, state, and federal laws are revised to meet today's land use realities.

Many laws and local ordinances are hopelessly outdated and unable to meet the planning needs of modern society. The postage stamp approach to zoning prevalent twenty years ago is still common. In postage stamp zoning, each property or group of properties is viewed independently. If a proposed use works within the area of the postage stamp, and buffering or some other form of separation is provided to the adjoining property, then the developer is entitled to the right of use.

Today our society has a greater awareness that properties or groups of properties do not work in isolation. We do not live in a postage stamp world. Postage stamp development can easily destroy the relationship between one part of a community and another, or in rural areas, whole ecosystems. Postage stamp zoning leads to the incremental devaluation of resources having tremendous public value.

What is a proponent's perceived short-term property right is society's loss of long-term resources.

It is also critical to remember that laws which promote public discussion of societal values are every bit as important as the laws protecting the proponent's property rights. Usually the proponent is economically motivated. He is annoyed whenever there is a hitch in the review process, or when someone makes a case against him that might eat into his economic reward.

The proponent might be the timber company that is only allowed to destroy half of a virgin forest instead of the whole, the developer who is allowed a lesser density than that which was proposed, the company that is deprived of the opportunity to harvest billions of dollars of oil in a wildlife refuge.

Preservation represents an opportunity that once lost will never be regained. Laws that promote public discussion and careful consideration of competing interests benefit society, and development opponents who use those laws should take great pride in their advocacy. There is no reason to apologize.

Finally, the proponent who accuses the opponent of drawing on irrelevant laws to make her case is a pot calling the kettle black. Proponents use every available legal tool to promote their projects. Why shouldn't opponents do the same?

Are there boundaries? Absolutely. You have to maintain intellectual honesty or you cannot expect more of anyone else. You may also make innocent property owners into victims without any legitimate justification. In 1997 an international company called Buquebus proposed a high-speed luxury ferry between Naples and Key West, Florida. The ferry was to have transported 300 passengers twice a day on a 175-foot-long-jet-propelled hydrofoil. The company contracted for the purchase of three parcels of land in the commercial waterfront district, parcels largely owned by long-time city residents who held a reasonable expectation of a right to use their property for commercially zoned, water dependent uses. All three parcels were located next to a major arterial roadway (U.S. 41) that carries up to 75,000 cars a day.

Notwithstanding the compliance of the proposal with the zoning ordinance and the support of the adjacent neighbors, the city staff determined that some of the property was in the noise overlay district for the Naples airport, which was part of the comprehensive plan. They made this determination even though adjacent property was not considered to be within the district, meaning, presumably, that it was less affected by airport noise; and even though the noise from the adjacent highway was far greater than any possible airport noise. The apparent purpose of the comprehensive plan provision was to discourage residential uses in airplane flight paths. The city staff determined that the proponents would have to rezone their property to a planned-development designation based solely on the comprehensive plan overlay for the airport. Despite such procedural hurdles, the proposal was approved by the city council on a first reading of the planned development ordinance, subject only to a second hearing.

The interim city attorney advised the city council that the ferry was an allowed use in the waterfront under the existing zoning designation (C-2A). The director of natural resources advised the council that he could not find any environmental objections to the proposal. Adjacent neighbors, both commercial property owners and condominium residents, voiced support for the proposal.

Several citizens groups then whipped the public into a frenzy, claiming that the ferry would carry passengers to Cuba, was out of scale with Naples' charm, and was too large for Naples Bay. Some of the opponents lived in the exclusive waterfront community of Port Royal, home of the rich and famous. Port Royal is also on Naples Bay; the ferry would pass many of the homes on its way to the gulf. Many Port Royal residents themselves have large yachts docked behind their homes.

After a public hearing that lasted over ten hours, the city council denied the petition for rezoning. The primary reasons for denial were the speculative impacts of the ferry on the bay and the additional fear of an influx of tourists, possibly from a foreign land. None of this had anything to do with airport noise, the original reason for the forced rezoning. Rather than attempt to regulate on the basis of a real concern—possible impacts to the bay—the city used a procedure of dubious legality to deny a land use that was clearly allowed as a matter of right. This was intellectually dishonest. The city clearly went too far, making innocent property owners into victims of arbitrary application of local laws.

Once you know the facts and have received advice from your professionals, it is time to develop positions that support your objectives. What are the strongest legal arguments you can make? What is the most appropriate procedure to follow in opposing the development proposal? These questions must be answered.

Choose the most publicly credible positions, for those will be most easily understood by decisionmakers and staff. Look at the development proposal in light of recent precedents established by the decisionmaking body. What positions have they taken in similar cases? This is very important. Positions should be prioritized accordingly.

Once a position is developed, it should be formalized. This can be done in several ways. Opponents may simply employ a position paper to be shared with all interested parties. If the opposition has enlisted the help of consultants, the position may be incorporated into written reports laying out all the facts and citing authoritative resources underpinning their expert opinion. If there is an attorney involved, the position should be formalized in a legal opinion letter to be shared directly with the municipal attorney.

In a formalized position, all arguments should be included, even if they do not promote priorities. What is not a priority argument today may become a priority argument tomorrow, when additional information surfaces. Then the written position should find its way into the hands of the proponent, municipal or agency staff, and decisionmakers. The law does not favor surprise. It is much better to come before decisionmakers at the final hearing with clean hands and an honest heart than to be caught trying, in effect, to ambush the proponent. If your arguments are valid, get them on the table early and often.

Part 3

EFFECTIVE DIALOGUE

CHAPTER 10

Communication and Public Relations

The first step in establishing dialogue is positive team communication: keeping members of the opposition informed as the development challenge unfolds. Communication is a vital part of the opposition effort, for it makes opponents feel as if they belong and are part of a coordinated group effort.

TEAM COMMUNICATION

In team communication, the proponent usually has a significant advantage over the opposition. The proponent's small team of professional consultants know how to communicate with each other—that is what they are paid, in part, to do. They are equipped with the computers and modems and fax machines to coordinate with one another. They stay informed daily.

In contrast, members of the opposition team, busy with their own jobs, typically see each other infrequently and communicate in a far less structured way. This is also true for any professional they hire, because the opposition file is usually only one of many on that person's desk.

Overcoming this disadvantage is a challenge, but being aware of it, opponents can actually make communication into a strength.

It is wiser, at the very outset of a land use confrontation, to devise a communication strategy. There are many available means: conversations, faxes, letters, newsletters, meetings, electronic mail, newspaper articles, radios spots, and so on. The opponents should decide which of these will best serve their needs. And in choosing, they should stress efficiency. Remember that potential opposition team members may work in highly demanding jobs. Volunteer work eats into time that would otherwise be spent with family or friends. Those who might lead the charge are probably used to acting quickly and decisively in their jobs. To attract talented members and leaders, the communication infrastructure has to accommodate their needs. It must accomplish and say the most with the least effort.

There are a number of communication strategies that will greatly help the opposition.

Don't call meetings just to meet.

Meetings should have a purpose. Too often opponents call meetings simply to convince themselves that they have a purpose. They feel as if they should be doing something, although they don't understand exactly what it is they should be doing. Therefore they meet. This is a big mistake.

When you call a meeting, it should have an agenda—a beginning, a middle, and an end. Shun the temptation to socialize, at least until after the meeting. Everyone present should be allowed to participate and leave as need be. Identify necessary decisions and make them. Above all, don't wander from topic to topic and back again.

One of the ironies in community representation is that organizations often emulate those government bureaucracies of which they are so critical. Avoid falling into the trap of floundering, or over-socializing, or over-meeting.

*Have opposition consultants advise
the opposition as a group when possible.*

It is often better that the members of opposition hear professional advice together as a group. This gives all opposition members access to unfiltered professional advice, which is better than having it passed from one team member to another, like the mistranslated message in the old game of telephone. When the opposition engages professionals, it should make sure that they update the entire group from time to time.

Disseminate information quickly.

The complexion of a land use battle changes day by day. It is important that every opponent keep abreast of late-breaking news. In today's world, that is not difficult. Faxes and e-mail can be simultaneously transmitted to many people. Opponents should emphasize speed over wording. A message delayed is often a message lost.

In an initial organizational meeting, obtain everyone's addresses, home telephone numbers, work numbers, fax numbers, and e-mail addresses. Then place this information in an address book for the benefit of all.

When important information surfaces, it should be immediately disseminated. This will keep all opponents focused and feeling that they are part of a well-coordinated team.

Use the media.

Newsletters can be an effective means of communicating, especially when the development proposal is moving slowly. Indeed, if your community association has several hundred members, a newsletter may be the only effective way to reach all of them with important information.

There are other useful media tools when the opposition membership is extremely large, time is short, and information must get out. However, if the media are used to reach opposition membership, the leaders won't have control of what information is reported. If the media get it wrong, the whole of the opposition will suffer the consequences. For that reason, direct communication is usually more effective.

Hire consultants knowledgeable with systems.

Presumably, you have hired consultants with communications skills. Consultants can greatly facilitate team coordination if they are organized and have up-to-date communications systems. If consultants can simultaneously disseminate information to many members of an opposition group, opponents may gain the communication advantage normally reserved to the proponent.

Use the Internet.

Community Internet sites now abound and Internet e-mail is readily available at no cost. Use it. Post information and develop community sites on the web that keep all citizens informed of pending proposals. If you need a place to start visit the web sites Neighborhood America.net.

PUBLIC RELATIONS

One of my law school professors, Zygmunt J. B. Plater, described print and broadcast media as the fourth arm of government. This is certainly true in land use battles, where the local media play a critical role. They create an environment of public accountability that fosters friendly resolution.

If it adheres to the principles of pure journalism, the local newspaper or radio station will report the facts of a land use problem in an unbiased manner. The media's role will be to educate the public about the particulars of a development proposal. And public education is critical to the opposition, for it is difficult to win a land use battle, whether through public hearing or negotiation, without popular support from the community. If you expect a politician to go out on a limb for you, you must be able to convince your fellow citizens of the merits of your opposition. Fair reporting is one good way to convince them.

Of course, it is a rare newspaper or radio station that divorces itself from editorial bias. The local beat reporter, often young and with limited experience, is acutely aware of the views of her editors. They have been around for a while and are more familiar with the dynamics of local decisionmaking. As hard as the reporter tries, her coverage of controversial land use proposals may well be colored. Editors and reporters aren't robots. They are human, and they tend to see things in a certain way. Their biases may be subtle (for instance, they may devote different amounts of space to differing points of view in a newspaper article) or they may be more blatant (as when they deliberately quote out of context). Often an editor will have a particular bias. As opponents, you should be aware of the bias because it will color the reporting.

You should also understand that reporters have a difficult challenge in reporting neighborhood conflicts, which can involve complicated technical engineering or scientific questions. Complex situations do not lend themselves to reporting in five hundred word articles, or thirty-second sound bites. The emotions stirred up by conflict are an easy subject for reporters, but emotions cloud objective analysis. Furthermore, facts tend to evolve throughout the life of a land proposal, so that reporters are constantly trying to hit a moving target. The reporter's job, to identify and report substance, to provide continuity in reporting, and to do it all objectively, is extremely difficult. This means that you should speak with reporters whom you trust to be precise and factual.

Opponents should follow basic rules when working with the media. Again, they must think strategically. Here are some guidelines:

1. Be conscious of timing.

Timing is important to communication. Should you approach the media when the opposition is launched, or later, closer to public hearings? There is no one rule that applies to every situation. Timing is a question of judgment. It should be decided with a clear understanding of potential risks and likely benefits.

For instance, if there is a possibility of a friendly resolution because the proponent does not want to expose herself to negative publicity, then involving the media early may ruin the opportunity for meaningful dialogue. The friendly resolution may be lost. Also, if there are still many facts to surface about the development proposal, approaching the media at this point may be self-defeating: your opposition will rest on incomplete facts.

However, there are certain compelling reasons to approach the media sooner rather than later. For instance, public explanation of the opponents' position may be the only way to force the proponent to the bargaining table. Likewise, if he holds his view with unshakable conviction, use of the media to tell the opposing story may be the only means of creating public accountability.

Also, if the proponent is already using the media to build support, then as opponents you should act accordingly. Approaching the media early creates credibility with reporters because it provides them with the opportunity for more educated and unbiased reporting. Reporters who follow a story will conduct more in-depth research than if they are left to reporting a single public hearing.

2. Be prepared and factual.

Opponents should make sure that they are armed with facts before approaching the media. You are not only shoring up your own position; you are giving the media the tools to critically question the proponent. Never say anything to a reporter which you do not know to be fact, and properly qualify all statements. The embarrassment of public mistakes can eat away at your credibility. If something is an opinion, call it an opinion. Don't call it a fact. Also, play back what you are going to say before you say it. Put yourself in the shoes of the reader or listener, and see if what you are about to say makes sense.

3. Be rational, not just emotional.

It doesn't serve your cause to act solely out of emotion. Most land use stories have a compelling emotional dimension. This should be apparent to the average reading public if the facts are properly presented. The public is smart. Most people will put themselves in your shoes. That doesn't mean you should be a robot. Simply temper your emotions, so that you won't be portrayed as arbitrary.

4. Avoid manipulation.

If you try to trick reporters, or the public, they will know it. Reporters are trained to be wary of manipulation. They have been burned before.

5. Use visual aids.

A picture is worth a thousand words. Recently in a coastal construction setback case I provided our local paper, the *Naples Daily News,* with a photograph of a building slab poured to the erosion control line, which under Florida law is defined as the mean high water line existing prior to any beach renourishment project. My clients were neighbors of the property owner pouring the slab, and their contention was that it did not observe an appropriate setback to the mean high water line. The photograph appeared on the front page of the local section of the *Naples Daily News*. It told the entire story and was more effective than the story itself. The general public could not imagine how a property owner could be allowed to build without a setback to the erosion control line. It was clear that the construction was in error.

Newspaper photographers are not always available and don't always understand a problem well enough to take the right photograph. If possible, provide the reporter with photographs clearly demonstrating the nature of the land use conflict.

6. *Avoid picking fights unnecessarily.*

Don't publicly lash out at the proponent, developer, government, or individuals representing the proponent. If they are being arbitrary, that will become apparent. The opposition's task is simply to describe the conflict in factual terms. In other words, take the high road.

7. *Choose your spokesperson wisely.*

The loudmouth in your opposition group who talks just to hear herself is not the person you want to speak with reporters. Should a professional spokesperson, such as your attorney, do your media liaison for you? In my opinion, lawyers are not the best spokespeople because the public tends to view them as hired guns whose comments have been paid for. They are cast as insincere. The benefit of having a lawyer for a spokesperson is that she will probably know what to say and, just as importantly, what not to say.

Consider the choice confronting residents of Hailey, Idaho, opposed to an agreement made by Idaho's Governor Batt. As reported by the *Wood River Journal* (April 14,1996), the agreement with the U.S. Department of Energy would allow the shipment of nuclear fuel to the Idaho National Engineering Laboratory, where it was to be stored for forty years. Many prominent Idaho residents opposed the agreement. One was the well-known actor Bruce Willis. Would he be the best spokesperson for the opposition?

Perhaps. His involvement would possibly give the issue regional or national publicity. The danger was that decisionmakers could typecast him, however unfairly.

The opposition elected to use Mr. Willis and his support in a visible way. Mr. Willis accompanied opponents to Boise, the state capital, and promptly gave interviews to all willing reporters. He was both sincere and articulate. He brought regional attention to a regional issue. Though it appears that the proposal is going ahead, choosing him as public spokesperson was clearly the correct choice. Remember, however, that fame does not always equal intelligence or effectiveness. Not in squabbles over land use.

8. Do not overexpose the opposition.

An intermittent stimulus creates a stronger bond with the community than a continual diet of negative opposition which will eventually start to sound like whining. Saying something to the media only when there is a purpose is a much more fruitful strategy. That way you won't lose your audience.

Taken together, these simple guidelines should help build good communication with the media. The media are an effective tool for public education, and public education is what wins community support and the hearts and minds of decisionmakers.

CHAPTER 11

Knowing and Communicating with the Proponent

Who is the mysterious entity behind the development proposal? Are its principals from another planet? Did they land in your community by accident, or design? Or are they like us, full of questions, concerns, and competing motivations?

Getting to know the proponent is a valuable tactic, one often overlooked by the opposition. To communicate effectively, to anticipate the proponent's arguments, to develop effective opposition strategies, and to reach a friendly resolution, you must first understand the proponent.

What is her educational and family background? Her experience in development? Has she had successes? Failures? Is she generally tolerant of differing views, or intolerant?

In what environment has the proponent developed projects? In a highly regulated environment, or one relatively free of regulation? This is important because proponents become accustomed to their surroundings. If a proponent who has limited her experience to the construction of suburban housing suddenly expands into a highly regulated environment with strict codes, she may have a difficult time adjusting. Her company is not accustomed to complying with regulations directed towards the community's needs rather than its own. On the other hand, if the proponent has generally developed communities in a highly regulated environment and she moves into a comparatively unregulated environment, she may bring with her a philosophy of raising development standards.

Opponents often balk at the idea of getting to know the proponent. It is almost always easier to generate support against the unknown, to play upon people's fears. Pinning the label "developer" or "bureaucrat" on the proponent will stir up negative connotations in the hearts and minds of citizens. Also, it is more difficult to engage a proponent in public warfare if he has an identity, a human side.

So who is the proponent, and what are her motivations? I have sketched four general personality types that are commonly encountered among proponents: the Romantic, the Cookie Cutter, the Bully, and the Professional Community Developer. My purpose isn't to stereotype, but rather to help readers understand how a given proponent is likely to act in the attempt to see her project through.

THE ROMANTIC

The Romantic is so in love with her project that she has convinced herself of its economic feasibility regardless of known risks. Often the Romantic will be an out-of-towner unfamiliar with local history and the peculiar dynamics of local economics.

Romantics often have economics of their own. They may be wealthy by most citizens' standards, but not wealthy enough for the equity funding of large-scale projects. Often because they are successful in their profession, they believe they can be successful in development.

The Romantic may be able to find a lender or group of rich professionals—athletes, doctors, lawyers—who will encourage her fantasy through third-party investment. The Romantic often plays with other people's money ("opm"), another factor that can interfere with decisionmaking. In this sense, government agen-

The Romantic

cies and political bodies may be the ultimate Romantics. Consider the rush to build professional sports stadiums in all parts of the country with taxpayer dollars. Romantics may have the dollars to put on a first-rate dog and pony show, but when it comes to performance, they don't measure up. The gap between reality and fantasy is visible in partially completed developments, or poor or badly maintained ones.

Communities, often starved for economic growth, are all too often willing to oblige Romantics' unrealistic expectations. Romantics like to schmooze, and their target communities, wanting to believe in the economic feasibility of development, respond accordingly. In this situation, decisionmakers ignore obvious flaws in the proposal. The community is saddled with the economic consequences and long-term planning issues in the wake of the failed development.

Romantics are not always proponent developers. They may be citizens' groups or government agencies advocating ill-conceived development decisions as well. The proposal to fill the Critical Wildlife Area on Sand Dollar Island is a good example. The citizen proponents are willing to ignore the probable loss of critical nesting habitats by bulldozing a barrier island at a cost of several million dollars, all to achieve a shorter walk to the beach.

The clear strategy for opposing the Romantic is a clear presentation of facts. Attack the Romantic's underlying assumptions and development economics. Make the Romantic work to justify each possible step.

THE COOKIE CUTTER

The Cookie Cutter may be a company or government agency that imposes itself on a community ignorant of its development standards. The Cookie Cutter, often from someplace else, mass produces its development choices.

The "box" store built for mass merchandising is an excellent example of cookie cutter development. When a mass merchandiser comes to town, it is with a predetermined mindset of what is needed to conduct business. The stores are built with preconceived dimensions, and in the most convenient locations—that is, wherever the greatest crowds can be drawn.

The Cookie Cutter's advance crew is trained to say all of the right things. It operates according to well defined rules and policies, regardless of whether those rules and policies meet community stan-

The Cookie Cutter

dards. The corporate advance team's challenge is to get the job done as expeditiously and cost-effectively as possible. Appease the natives and get on with business. This approach does not lead to the best land use decisions because generic standards are often out of harmony with local development standards and the fabric of neighborhoods.

Government agencies are all too prone to playing the role of the cookie cutter. Take the Florida Department of Transportation (FDOT). It has adopted what are known as access management regulations. The articulated purpose of these regulations is to create higher capacity on local highways—that is, to move more cars faster. The FDOT supposedly accomplishes this purpose by limiting the number of driveways and median openings allowed for businesses. In urban areas, the FDOT moves traffic on local roads at higher speeds by building dividing walls between different parts of the community. Because people can't get across major arterial roads, local roads effectively become expressways. The FDOT executes its mission regardless of whether local communities would prefer slower moving traffic and neighborhoods that function together rather than apart.

Another good example are the telecommunications companies which are currently advocating the proliferation of cell towers and transmission facilities throughout the country regardless of local desires or needs. These towers dot local rights of way, often dramatically lowering property values and dooming the public landscape to utilitarian mediocrity. These companies have gone so far as to request federal preemption of local development decisions by asking the Federal Communications Commission to adopt rules taking away communities' rights to regulate these facilities. In their eyes, one size fits all.

The most successful strategy for defending against the Cookie Cutter is to educate him about community values. Remember, the Cookie Cutter probably won't have an economic interest in the outcome of land use choices. Unlike other proponents he will receive a paycheck, win, lose, or draw. Sooner or later he will give in the philosophical tug of war.

THE BULLY

The Bully uses brute force to get what he wants. Community issues are secondary to him. The Bully believes that he is advancing community interest by advancing his own economic interest. Contextual development means nothing to the Bully—except as something that might threaten his profit.

The Bully

The Bully tends to be litigious. If you encounter a developer or government agency with a track record of litigation, chances are you have a Bully on your hands. The ultimate Bully intimidates citizen groups with what are known as SLAPP suits. These are slander and libel lawsuits brought against such groups to discourage public comment and opposition. Though they are virtually never successful, all too often the prospect of a suit causes citizens to back down. Who wants to get roped into a lawsuit for speaking out in a public forum?

The only strategy for dealing with a Bully is to hit him in the nose. The Bully understands one thing and one thing only, opposing force. You have to get the Bully's attention. The way to do this is to make him understand that you are well funded, well organized, prepared and committed. All this will translate into increased time and cost for the Bully, something he will understand.

THE PROFESSIONAL COMMUNITY DEVELOPER

The Professional Community Developer is a member of your community and therefore committed to its long-term health. She usually has a proven track record of projects. This proponent has little interest in overreaching, because her reputation is at stake and because she cares about the economic health of the community. The highest-quality development tends to come out of negotiations between the community and the Professional Community Developer, who is sympathetic to community vision. Often the Professional Community Developer lives in the community. The strategy with this person, then, is personal negotiation.

Of course, the personality traits described above are only reference points. A proponent may be one part Romantic, one part Cookie Cutter, one part Bully, and one part Professional Community Developer. Strategies of opposition usually have to be varied accordingly.

Keep in mind that Romantics, Cookie Cutters, and Bullies will almost always try to cast themselves as Professional Community Developers. They will say all the right things, usually sincerely: "We want to be good neighbors." "We are here for the long term." In the final analysis, action will tell.

In addition to understanding the proponent's personality, the opposition must make an effort to understand the economics of a given proposal. Otherwise it will be difficult to evaluate the proponent's motivations and the viability of her project. The central question is this: Is the proponent an End User or a Flipper?

END USERS AND FLIPPERS

An End User is a proponent who proceeds with development for a potentially profitable purpose unrelated to land itself. McDonald's is not a real estate development company. It is a food company. It makes money selling burgers. It is an End User.

In contrast, a Flipper is a proponent whose intention is to create value by obtaining government approvals, then selling property to an End User with the zoning or development rights in place. The Flipper acquires property, creates development rights, and then flips them to an End User. Effectively, the Flipper is paid to undertake the risk of development application.

Why does it make a difference whether a proponent is an End User or a Flipper? Because the End User will care about how the development choice relates to its surroundings and how it is perceived in the eyes of the community. The End User stands a better chance of profit if she is also a good neighbor.

Because the Flipper has no intention of developing the property, he is less sensitive to community needs. He won't be around when final development occurs. Furthermore, every dollar that goes to development dedications or community amenities directly reduces the economic reward of the Flipper. An End User will only pay for the economic potential of the end use, not the amenities. Therefore the Flipper has little motivation to make a proposed development more compatible with community standards.

> ## DEVELOPER DEDICATIONS
>
> Developer dedications are promises developers often make during a zoning approval process to try to lessen the public impact of a project. Examples of such promises might be dedicating land for a public park, or constructing a road or sidewalk. Dedications are of benefit to the general public, not only the residents of the future development.

A further contrast is that the End User has a well-defined target. It knows exactly what is or is not economically feasible. The Flipper, on the other hand, merely has a development idea. This leads to a common pattern of public dialogue in which a Flipper promotes a given project that is not economically feasible. When the End User arrives on the scene, his first course of action is to modify the Flipper's development approvals to make them economically viable.

Very often, opponents who think they have won by securing development commitments from a Flipper end up confronting an End User's subsequent application for modification. The battle must

103

be fought all over again. At this point, unfortunately, opponents may have been depleted of their resources in the battle against the Flipper's development fantasy.

Government proponents are rarely Flippers. When they propose development they are almost always End Users. Their development choices—building roads, schools, parks, and so on—are motivated by the desire to fulfill a public need.

Romantics often end up being Flippers. Unable to finance their fantasy development, they are forced to sell to End Users who have a more pragmatic, economically feasible project.

Cookie Cutters are typically End Users. They make money or achieve a public purpose as an incident to the development choice, not because they are in the business of land development. For instance, chain restaurants make money in their operations, not because they zone and sell property.

Bullies can be Flippers or End Users. Bullies will generally pursue profit in any fashion available. If that means zoning and flipping property, they will do that. If that means zoning, building, and developing, they will do that.

Professional Community Developers are rarely Flippers. They tend to devote themselves to community-sensitive development.

For opponents, there is greater certainty in working with a proponent who is also an End User. The End User's agreements are more reliable than the Flipper's. When opponents face a Flipper, they will also face another development proposal, and perhaps one after that.

So we return to the question with which we began: Who is the proponent? Is he a Romantic? A Cookie Cutter? A Bully? A Professional Community Developer? And what is his economic motivation? Is he an End User or a Flipper? For opponents, the answers to these questions will determine how much faith they should place in development commitments and resolutions that are signed. Will proposals return in a different form later? If you know the proponent, you can communicate with her. Thoughtful communication builds trust, credibility, and mutual respect, the foundation for a friendly resolution.

Hasty, spontaneous communication breeds mistrust and virtually guarantees public confrontation. So there are real benefits to understanding the art of communicating with the proponent.

In communicating with the proponent you should have a strategic purpose—a clear idea of what you want to achieve with each exchange, what should be said, and what should not be said. There are four basic reasons for communicating with the proponent:

Obtaining information from the proponent;
Gaining credibility by showing that you are prepared;
Educating the proponent;
Negotiating.

Let's consider the case of neighbor versus neighbor. You believe you ought to be able to speak with the proponent. After all, you are neighbors. You shouldn't have to hire an attorney to resolve neighborhood problems.

Say that your neighbor plans to build his house in a way that blocks your view. Or maybe he decides to use his home for a commercial enterprise, such as a child care facility, under the guise of a "home occupation." The first you hear of it is when someone begins clearing the lot next door, or in the case of the child care center, begins installing industrial strength playground equipment. Should you talk to the neighbor? The answer is probably yes. But what should you say? The purpose of your initial conversation should be to learn exactly what he plans, no more, no less. You are obtaining information.

Your instinctive reaction might be to express objections. This of course guarantees that the proponent will place himself on guard, and then you will have to work for your information. Or you might indicate that you aren't opposed to your neighbor's plans as described to you. Then later you come before a planning commission, city or county council, or judge and your neighbor is arguing equities: "Your Honor, I talked to her and she indicated that everything was okay. Now after I have built, she objects." In other words, the proponent neighbor argues that you have waived any rights you might have.

If you talk to the neighbor, obtain as much information as possible. Express your interest and concern. Then express reservation: you intend to think about it and talk further. Try this: "I want to be a good neighbor, but I am concerned. I have my life savings or substantial worth invested in my house and I want to make sure that it is not affected." You have left the door open for structured negotiation.

Let's try another example in a broader context. A citizens' group meets directly with the proponent developer with no representation. The opponents completely expose their goals. They dominate the meeting with a recitation of their position. But they don't listen. Now the proponent knows everything about the opponents while the opponents know nothing about the proponent.

An opposition member, naïve about the politics of land use, tells the developer everything about the opposition group, such as its limited membership and resources. The developer quickly surmises her ability to outlast the opposition on financial resources alone.

Or perhaps an opposition member decides to intimidate the developer—"I'll take you all the way to the Supreme Court." This sort of blustering can quickly close channels for further negotiation. It convinces the proponent that the blusterer is a neighborhood nut. Used to such types—they are an occupational nuisance—she is prepared to hold her ground. The proponent will not be intimidated.

Or one of the group feels the need to "rush to the altar." Often by hurrying negotiations, opposition members sell themselves short and achieve a less than ideal resolution.

In communicating with the proponent there should never be statements of position, only questions. Take the Columbo approach. Keep asking questions, and listen! If the answers to your questions justify your worst fears, then you should strongly consider obtaining legal advice before further communication. Moreover, any further communication ought to be structured. That way you'll gain credibility.

For instance, you could ask the proponent if your consultants, whether they are architects, engineers, or planners, might directly communicate with hers. This way, you gather information while showing the proponent that you are both smart and prepared.

As for educating the proponent, this is the only way to make real progress and reach meaningful compromise. Most development proposals present the opportunity to educate proponents as well as opponents, decisionmakers, and the general citizenry. And education is how positive change occurs.

Perhaps you know something, some scientific fact, some planning concept, some resulting condition, which is not readily apparent to the proponent. Perhaps the proponent is willing to learn, which may well be the case if she is a member of the community. Ignoring facts and results is not publicly acceptable behavior, nor is it necessarily in the proponent's self-interest.

For instance, in the case of the segmented breakwater construction described in chapter 7, what if the opponents could have educated supporters of the breakwaters to the obvious dangers of their installation? What if the opponents could have convinced beach front homeowners that the installation of breakwaters might actually accelerate erosion of beach front property, the exact opposite of what was desired?

Most proponents will at least listen. And if you, as opponents, have a well researched position based on solid scientific and professional opinion, proponents gain little by being blind to it.

Once you discover everything possible about the proposal you will be in a position to negotiate. Allow me to share several guidelines for negotiation that should give you confidence. Of course, there are abundant manuals on the art of negotiation. However, these pointers are specifically targeted at land development negotiations.

1. Choose an effective leader as your spokesperson.

The first challenge of negotiation is to have the right citizens doing the talking. The opposition must choose a leader who is capable of negotiation. This may or may not be a clear choice. Often the most capable person is the most reluctant.

Negotiation requires skill, knowing how to relate to the people sitting on the other side of the table, knowing what to ask for, knowing when to be firm and when to compromise.

Negotiation by committee tends to lose focus. However, frequently there is room for more than one spokesperson. A duo consisting of the good guy and the bad guy, one being reasonable, the other firm and more aggressive, can be effective. Or team an analytical diplomat with a person who is the emotional voice of the opposition.

2. Allow the proponent to open negotiations.

Why? Because you will learn more that way. When proponents start the discussion, they have a responsibility to bring something to the table, even if it is only an explanation of their view of the merits of the development proposal.

3. Conduct negotiations in a familiar setting.

Members of the opposition will feel much more comfortable and be much more effective negotiating in their own environment. Whenever possible, have the proponent and her representatives come to one of your offices or your group meeting place. Don't feel that you must meet in the proponent's territory.

4. Beware of the "end around" play.

The end around is that well known football play in which the entire offense (the proponent) travels toward one side of the field, luring the defense (the opposition) into following. At the same time the quarterback hands off to the end, who runs to the vacated part of the field and scores.

The land-use equivalent takes place when the proponent initiates discussions with neighbors or community groups of his choice. He ignores other citizens who may have stronger or more enlightened views. Upon reaching agreement with the group of his choice, he then announces that he has "met with the neighbors" and fulfilled his responsibility of communication. The proponent runs to the open field and scores, obtaining the approvals he needs.

If you see the proponent pulling this trick, send a notice letter as described in chapter 7. The notice letter alerts everyone, including the proponent, of your concern. It pre-empts the end run.

5. *Put agreements in writing.*

If communication leads to even incremental agreements, put them in writing, even if it is only in the form of a confirming letter. Create a record of communications. This will be very important when the proponent's representatives are standing before decisionmakers claiming that this is the first they've heard of the opposition's willingness to compromise. Certainly, had they known sooner, they would have pursued discussions. Now, at the point of decision, it is too late. Committing agreements to paper keeps everyone honest.

6. *Don't be bought.*

Remember the old science fiction film where the aliens land on Earth and promise Earthlings a better life on the aliens' home planet? After wining and dining the Earthlings, they persuade them to make the journey. The Earthlings are whisked off to the home planet only to discover that they are the solution to the aliens' food shortage.

Even the best public relations strategy should be reviewed critically. If a land use decision makes sense, go with it. If it doesn't, no amount of "up front" money and financial promises will make up for the negative effects of the development choice. Don't be eaten alive by living for the here and now. Development choices must withstand the test of time.

What will your community do if a development proponent is sold, or files bankruptcy? So much for the payments. Residents will be stuck with the development choice. Today's public relations is tomorrow's smoke. Decide land use issues on their merits. Don't be bought.

Understanding how to relate to and negotiate with the proponent is not always easy, especially for those who are unfamiliar with the process of land use challenge. However, if you, as opponents, remember the strategic purposes of communication, and supplement them with the negotiation guidelines described above, you will greatly improve your chances of success.

CHAPTER 12

The Friendly Resolution

Effective dialogue lays the groundwork for the friendly resolution, where all parties are satisfied, or equally dissatisfied but willing to stop there. Friendly resolutions are negotiated compromises sensitive to the needs of proponents, opponents, and the public.

Friendly resolutions generate long-lasting understanding between proponents and opponents. With a friendly resolution comes a measure of certainty. With a friendly resolution come savings of time and money. With a friendly resolution comes peace.

The value of the friendly resolution cannot be underestimated. It often allows resources that were to be used for the fight to be used for the development of an alternative land use plan, or to enhance the quality of the development choice. The friendly resolution brings what might otherwise be a noncontextual development more into harmony with its surroundings, and perhaps makes it more acceptable to the community.

For opponents, the friendly resolution may bring benefits not legally required of the proponent—for instance, dedications such as a sidewalk, landscaping, better drainage and water management, lighting, or public access to a natural resource such as a beach, forest, or park. Such measures enhance both the quality of the development and perhaps the surrounding community.

Communication among the proponent, the opposition, and the press is vital to the friendly resolution. Also vital is a willingness to listen and address the legitimate needs of the other side. This is especially difficult because, unlike other forms of negotiation, land use negotiation usually involves collective impacts, not discrete and easily defined issues. It also involves personalities with different backgrounds and economic interests.

Proponents must be willing to recognize and address legitimate community, neighborhood, or business concerns, while opponents must be willing to accept legal and economic realities. It is true that certain proposed land uses are so inappropriate that opponents can be reasonably sure of success. But what about the next proposal, and the one after that? At some point the question of what a given proponent can do with her property will be resolved. There are times when opponents accomplish more by working with a proponent who is willing to solve problems than by awaiting a future proponent who may not exhibit the same sensitivity.

It is not unusual for a community to reject a slightly noncontextual proposal from a Professional Community Developer who has a strong interest in the long-term health of a community, only to be saddled with a Bully whose more theoretically contextual proposal has limited economic viability. Not working with the friend ensures a worse result from a foe.

The same can be said of proponents. Often they have encountered such fierce opposition from communities that they fight to just fight. Proponents can be rugged individualists who seize any opportunity to defend their perceived property rights. Most proponents, however, understand that the economic cost of plan improvement is far less than the economic cost of public warfare. Perhaps more importantly, plan improvements do serve the proponent's long-term interest. For developers, the best marketing may begin in the most obvious place, with the neighbors.

Like any successful negotiation, the friendly resolution confers mutual advantage. If proponents and opponents alike perceive the advantage of measures that improve the quality of the development choice, then a friendly resolution is possible.

The most lasting friendly resolutions occur when there is trust and cooperation. Proponent and opponents alike must understand each other enough to have confidence that any agreement made will be honored.

Often friendly resolutions falter, not because of an absence of planning ideas that would fulfill the needs of all parties, but because proponents and opponents effectively speak different languages. Proponents are comfortable with businesslike talk, but restless when opponents come to the negotiating table full of local anecdotes. Proponents tend to view the opponents' requests as emotional, not rational.

Conversely, opponents don't easily grasp the murky parlance of development economics or public finance. They eye the proponent with distrust because they can't understand him.

It is not a coincidence that successful proponents are those who understand the needs, language, and structure of neighborhoods and neighborhood organizations. It is also not a coincidence that the neighborhoods most successful at guiding development are those that speak with a unified, businesslike voice. They are able to express their objectives in economic terms. Occasionally, there is a translator present, perhaps a political representative who speaks both languages.

Can both sides win? Are all conflicts capable of resolution? Let's consider several examples.

As reported by the *Aspen Times* (July 1, 1996), a local skiing company proposed to use water from Snowmass Creek to make snow for its resort at Snowmass Mountain. This seemed reasonable: skiers need snow, Mother Nature doesn't always cooperate, and skiing is the predominant industry in Aspen, the livelihood of many citizens.

However, the proposal triggered opposition from the Aspen Wilderness Workshop and the Snowmass Capitol Creek Coalition. Changing flow would affect the stream's ecology. The decisionmaking body in this controversy was the Colorado Water Conservation Board (CWCB).

In 1992 the Aspen Wilderness Workshop brought a lawsuit against the CWCB on a prior decision to allow stream-flow reduction. After thousands of dollars in expenses, the Workshop won before the Colorado Supreme Court because of a procedural error that nullified proponent permits allowing reduction of the stream flow. In 1996, the proponent and opposition came to an agreement: the proponent could use water from the stream, the amount depending on the creek's ability to accommodate flow reduction in any given year. The parties achieved a friendly resolution, saving thousands of dollars each. Both proponents and opponents received something. Both won.

If achievable, the friendly resolution should be pursued. But what happens when a land use proposal is so out of context that no amount of short-term education by either proponent or opponent will bridge the gap between what to each are important principles?

Consider a case reported by the *New York Times* (April 21, 1996) involving proposed logging of the Headwaters Grove redwoods in northern California. The 189,000 acres of timber represent the largest stand of redwoods outside of publicly owned lands in the United States. The logging was proposed on the basis of principle. The developer, a paper company, believes in its constitutional right to use its property, regardless of the cost in precious virgin forest. After all, each redwood is worth over $100,000. In the eyes of environmentalists, the paper company has a moral responsibility to preserve the hardwoods. Once lost, they and all living things dependent on them are gone. These are two fundamentally different values between which society must choose. The final outcome of this conflict is still pending.

There are also many projects where compromise is not practical. No amount of buffering, lighting deflection, or fencing will mitigate the intrusive impact of some development. The hotly contested proposal to build a landfill atop Hobbs Mountain in northwestern Arkansas is a good example. According to the *Northwest Arkansas Times* (April 30, 1996), local representatives promised to keep a two-mile buffer to mitigate the development's impact on the surrounding area. Environmentalists and neighbors who have been fighting the proposal since 1989 understand that the effects of the landfill would extend well beyond two miles, and that the development would seriously harm the ecosystem of the Hobbs Mountain area. The landfill would destine the course of the area for years to come.

On a more limited scale, once a neighbor destroys an adjacent neighbor's view, the harm is done. One will create value at the expense of the other. Here is a clear choice not subject to compromise: Allow construction or don't.

Reaching a friendly resolution requires special wisdom on all sides of the negotiating table. A certain "win" today is not always better than a solution reached by compromise. The win may be temporary. The compromise is final.

On occasion, no one on either side of the table is reasonable, regardless of the wisdom of compromise. Both parties become gamblers willing to take their chances in the forum of public decisionmaking.

The message to development opponents is simple: Strive for friendly resolution, but prepare for battle.

Part 4

BATTLES IN THE PUBLIC EYE

CHAPTER 13

Preparation Wins

*W*hen the friendly resolution becomes an elusive, moving target of wistful hope, public confrontation may be unavoidable. In this case, opponents must know the rules of public battle. Most important is to understand that preparation wins.

The most effective preparation for public hearings is a quick start. Don't, by clinging to the last dangling thread of hope for settlement, place the opposition in a position of weakness. Opposition groups in denial will frequently wait until several days before a planning commission, municipal, or agency hearing before they fully prepare. By then it may be too late. Opponents are already in a position of significant disadvantage. Experts cannot be found. Information cannot be gathered. Neighbors who might be helpful to the cause are out of town or unavailable. As any coach or conductor knows, when it is time to perform, you play the way you practice.

In addition to getting off to a quick start, it's a good idea to anticipate how a proponent will present her case. What will she and her professionals say in support of the development proposal? The central themes of most proponent arguments are predictable. The proponent has certain development rights. She has been responsive to neighborhood concerns. She is merely advancing a plan that has been fully reviewed by staff. She is only asking for treatment that has previously been accorded to other applicants. Her arguments are supported by sound engineering and scientific studies and planning. These themes can be discovered in municipal staff files and in proponent's submittals. As described in chapter 7, the opposition must have copies of all proponent submissions until the day of the public hearing. Be careful: you don't want materials to be submitted to the decisionmakers' staff at the last minute without your knowledge.

How will the proponent advance these themes? Here opponents must understand the proponent's strategy. This is also predictable.

The government staff is responsible for making an independent assessment of the facts and arguments presented by the proponent. The proponent's objective is to obtain a favorable staff or agency report and then, in a sense, allow the staff to make his case for him. The proponent will also likely create legal barriers before any public hearings, perhaps by sending legal opinions in writing to the government attorney. Obtain copies of any such correspondence. Expect the proponent to fully assert his legal position.

Instead of vivid pictures demonstrating out-of-context results, the proponent will usually provide decisionmakers with fuzzy blue-line drawings or brightly colored concept plans. It is difficult to create a true picture of noncontextual results from these materials unless you are professionally trained to read such documents.

Imprecise visuals are a sophisticated camouflage. Proponent developers generally know how to use precise electronic visualization when it meets their needs, for example in engineering and marketing. They may spend hundreds of thousands of dollars in electronic images to hone design or to sell units to prospective buyers. Proponents could just as easily use these electronic images to demonstrate the contextual results of their proposals, but they won't if they know, privately, that those results would be negative.

Chances are the proponent will also rely on generalizations about the benefits of her project to the community, and that she will refer to her property rights. So how should you develop your opposition argument? The following steps will help you put together a winning argument.

1. Make an independent assessment of facts.

We've already discussed fact finding. Let me add that you should not blindly accept the proponent's facts. Challenge them. Are they correct? Are the proponent's scientific, engineering, or planning conclusions based on accurate assumptions? Is there room for *more* than one expert opinion? This is where opponents' consultants are on the stage. A related question is whether there might be alternative designs or solutions which might meet the proponent's objectives.

2. Question fundamental policy assumptions.

What about the policy assumptions underlying the proponent's arguments? The proponent often consciously chooses not to argue policy. His case will rest on the inherent assumption that building, construction, and growth are all positive economic objectives that he has a right to pursue.

Allow me to use an example: the proposed construction of a turnpike ramp off I-90 into the Boston Chinatown community (*Boston Globe,* April 30, 1996). In making the proposal, the transportation engineers working for the Massachusetts Turnpike Authority fulfilled their "mission"—the creation of "capacity" in the roadway system. In the engineers' view, such proposals move cars from point A to point B more efficiently. By making the proposal they are doing what, as a society, we have prescribed as their role. However, many residents of Chinatown believed that the ramp would route 25,000 cars per day through their community, destroying its character. The opposition group challenged the fundamental presumption of policy: that increased road capacity is always desirable, even when there are competing goals. Moving cars from point

A to point B faster—in engineering jargon, at a higher level of service (LOS)—is not always preferable where there is even a small chance that working neighborhoods and businesses might be harmed or destroyed. This is the argument which was advanced by the opponents of the turnpike exit and which ultimately carried the day. Opponents identified the proponent's policy assumptions and successfully challenged them (*Boston Globe,* June 25, 1997).

In similar cases successful opposition may require hiring experts with backgrounds different from those of the proponent's team. For instance, in cases like the turnpike expansion, perhaps the opposition should consider hiring a certified planner. The planner's mission and skills will be different from the transportation engineer's. Planners will try to reconcile competing values. How does the road relate to the community? The transportation engineer's emphasis will be capacity and volume. How many cars can move how fast through the pipeline? Deliberately slowing cars down or reducing capacity is engineering heresy.

Economists or appraisers might also be helpful in giving concrete testimony about diminished land values and economic loss in the wake of a development. The proponent will argue abstract economic gain. There are perhaps more vivid and tangible potential economic losses. This is true with almost all large public works projects.

Consider the matter of ballparks for major league sports franchises. In many cities major league teams threaten to move without public funding of construction, usually at a cost measured in the hundreds of millions of dollars. New York, Houston, Cleveland, and Miami are but a few of the cities that have recently endured the argument of financial plight.

Presumably the owners are successful businesspeople. Can't they find another way of ensuring long-term success? Do they really have to pay 25 ballplayers $25 to $50 million a year while claiming that there's not enough money to renovate existing stadiums? Instead, they panic and rush to build stadiums with little regard for the impact on surrounding neighborhoods.

Stadiums and ball teams are glamorous. All politicians talk about neighborhoods. The politician who can negotiate the big ballpark deal with the "heavy hitters" stands out in the crowd.

The opponents of ill-advised stadiums might add economic impact statements of their own to the debate. They might try this argument: "Subsidies to professional ball teams are a transfer of wealth from the public coffers to a few corporations and wealthy people who own franchises. Let's take the public dollars and invest them in our neighborhoods by creating landscaped parks, better lighting, and neighborhood plans, all competing land use choices. Or perhaps we could better invest the money in new schools to revitalize our neighborhood, spreading the resources more democratically. The economic benefit to our community which will flow from public investment in our neighborhoods is estimated to be equal to X + $10 million. The high-paying and skilled positions created within the private and public sectors will be equal to Y+200 jobs. X and Y are the purported economic benefits and job creation of the stadium proposal. As a community, let's work from a position of strength of accomplishment, not fear of loss."

Stadium proposals and similar public works projects undoubtedly have tangible economic benefits. It is hard to spend $100 to $300 million and not realize some public benefit. However, if the public discussion were cast in different terms, a contrast of alternatives, it would result in a better land use decision. Though the sports industry would have to adjust, it would survive and most cities would retain the economic benefit of sports facilities at lower cost and in more harmonious ways. In a choice between allowing citizens to maintain their homes and communities and providing opportunities for a few to enjoy a more plush sky box, the outcome should not be that challenging. The choice must be defined in clear-cut terms.

The point is, don't limit yourself to opposition on the proponent's terms by accepting his underlying assumptions and then conducting the debate in his language. Develop your own analysis by developing equally tangible alternatives.

3. Demonstrate a community of opposition to the decisionmakers.

There are many ways to do this, for example through petitions, letter writing, and marches. Many groups call local radio talk show programs to push specific issues into the public forum.

4. Prepare visuals.

By using visuals, opponents can show what proponents frequently attempt to hide or avoid: the undesirable effects of proposed development. Visuals should show what the noncontextual development would actually look like. They might do this with photographs, videotapes, two-dimensional, drawings or electronic images. Three-dimensional electronic images are especially effective, and the cost of producing them is now reasonable.

5. Research precedents.

It is probable that similar development proposals have been made within or near your own community. If not, perhaps the same proponent implemented a development in a faraway community but in a related context. If the precedent argues for your position, demonstrate the similarities. In the event that the example argues against the proposal, then define the differences and point out why it wouldn't work.

6. Put your position in writing.

As opponents, you should put your position in writing, share it with the municipal or agency attorney before any public hearings, and be prepared to make written positions part of the record. In the event that you are unable to complete your verbal presentation, the written position will preserve your rights of appeal.

PRESERVATION OF RIGHTS

Preserving the right to appeal is often overlooked during preparation. Most states follow a legal rule under which appeals to courts are limited to objections that are in the record of the public hearing. If you snooze, you lose.

7. Coordinate your presentation.

Coordinate your presentation while remaining flexible. You must know who is going to say what, when, and how. When preparing for your presentation, it helps to imagine yourself in the public hearing. It also helps to be familiar with the meeting facilities. Who is going to sit (or stand) where? Do you have all the equipment you need? Does it work? Where do the decisionmakers sit, and what are their names in order?

8. Ask this question:
Will the proposed development choice withstand the test of time?

Most importantly, arguments should be prepared for this ultimate question. Related questions might be: Will the development rule out the future well-being of others? Will a neighbor's view be hampered by that of future development, that of the neighbors? Will the choice mean that a neighboring business might go out of business, not because of competition but because the business is incompatible with the proposed development? Does the proposed choice take advantage of all opportunities for improvement? Does the choice take into account the functional life of the proposal, or the lifetime of its impacts? Does the choice take advantage of existing infrastructure?

How many times have you heard the fatalistic phrase "growth is inevitable" put forth by development proponents? In truth, much development is driven not by growth, but rather by convenience. It is easier to focus on short-term gain than long-term loss. In your preparation highlight this argument. Constantly return to the theme: *Will the proposed development choice withstand the test of time?* Ask and answer each of its component questions.

Proponents, opponents, and decisionmakers tend to concentrate on the short term. But development decisions have lasting effect. The building approved today will be in place thirty years from now. Opponents are consumed by what a choice might mean to their own self-interest. What will the choice mean to the next generation of residents, and the generation after that? Will the choice create a problem left for them to solve?

Consider the issue of nuclear waste storage at Yucca Mountain in Nevada. Government scientists say they can design a storage facility that will hold seventy thousand tons of spent nuclear waste and that will last at least ten thousand years (*Scientific American,* June 1996). The citizens of Nevada aren't so sure. They are preparing their own studies, studies which question the geologic stability of the mountain and ask the most basic questions. What if the government scientists are wrong? What if the unthinkable happens? Will the development choice withstand the test of time?

Or consider these, or any number of issues mentioned in your daily paper: If the State of Utah is allowed to buy federal public land for development, is the public better served than if that land remains under the management of the National Park Service? Are the citizens of Kansas better off in the long run saving the Haskell Baker wetlands, or allowing construction of the proposed South Lawrence Traffic Way? Is allowing the construction of a landfill on Hobbs Mountain in Arkansas today's solution but tomorrow's nightmare?

STRENGTH IN THE FACE OF ADVERSITY

Just before public hearings, opponents should individually and collectively take a deep breath and reflect on exactly how they are going to make the best presentation. Where is the energy going to come from? How will you maintain a positive attitude, regardless of adversity? I would suggest two avenues: one, know your respective roles and play them with confidence; and two, stay focused.

Each opponent should play the role consistent with his or her character. When people are asked to act out of character, they do and say unpredictable things which can hurt the opposition. The soft-spoken group member who leads the charge in the public hearing is not going to stir the enthusiasm of opponents or decisionmakers. Likewise, the member with an aggressive, hair-trigger temper may not convey the proper sense of diplomacy. Yet both people can have an important part in a public hearing. They act as foils to one another and define the boundaries of public discussion.

Miscasting citizens in public hearings can have comical results. The young adult who speaks with authority about his life experiences—"In my experience," "I have been here all of my life"—isn't going to be very credible. Youth should speak to the future. They should remind decisionmakers that they are making choices that will affect the community down the road. A better tack for a young adult is to ask the decisionmaker whether the proposal will allow the speaker the same opportunities that previous generations had. Will she be able to enjoy unspoiled habitats, beach access, mountain vistas, clean water? The youthful question puts decisionmakers in mind of their own youth, when perhaps they were asking the same questions.

The lawyer wannabe who quotes chapter and verse of statutes, cases, and state and federal constitutions is equally ineffective. ("You don't have a right to make this decision." "What you are doing is illegal." "This is unconstitutional.") Suggestion: Stay away from specific legal principles and emphasize policy and common sense results. All laws are ideally grounded in a legislator's view of the common good. Rather than argue the law, which will invite quick retorts from municipal attorneys whose territory you are invading, argue the common sense position which should underlie the law. Let attorneys fight the legal battles.

What about the recent arrival who wants to cast her new home in the mold of her former (and by inference, better) one: "The way we did it up north." Suggestion: Just describe the idea. Its origins are irrelevant. Nobody cares how you did it up north, or down south, or in the east or out west. You are here now.

That doesn't mean that your ideas don't represent a significant contribution. They may be grounded in state of the art planning and science. You may cite examples for comparison, but don't cast yourself as a foreigner. Most communities are ethnocentric. It is natural for decisionmakers to bristle at outside ideas. Cast yourself as a member of the community who has the potential to help with local planning.

Then there are the obviously influential leaders who play down to the audience, such as the state legislator who announces, "I am just appearing as an interested neighbor." Suggestion: Make points that are consistent with your background. If you are a state legislator or an accomplished community leader, don't be embarrassingly and insincerely humble before local, state, or federal decisionmakers.

The most successful presentations are sincere, thoughtful, and well prepared. Present yourself for who you are. And do it with confidence. Confidence is a friend of conviction, not its twin sister. Conviction is the belief in your cause. Confidence is belief in yourself. If you have doubts, they will be apparent to all. Remember, you are facing an issue that will shape the future of your home, business, or community. You belong at the public podium. Never, ever apologize for participating. That's what democracy is all about.

In the science fiction trilogy "Star Wars," the hero, Luke Skywalker, battled the Evil Empire by finding "the Force." The Force was a concentrated spiritual energy that allowed Skywalker to stay focused in the face of incredible adversity.

Citizens should approach opposition with the energy of Luke Skywalker. With proper focus and singular purpose, citizens are capable of staving off or moderating inappropriate land use proposals. It isn't easy to maintain focus. Land use conflicts involve many pilots with different missions. The engineer wants his road. The politician wants her public stadium. The developer wants his density. The logging company wants its lumber. The community wants its economic vitality. The neighborhood wants its tranquillity and harmony.

With so many competing interests, the pressures are immense. If you as a citizen question a popular project, you might be ostracized. If you're in a battle with your neighbors, and you win, you still have to live next door to them. Your children may go to school with the proponent's. You may attend the same church as the proponent's consultants. You may be members of the same country club. Naturally, people are reluctant to confront development issues when to do so would bring them up against friends or neighbors. Most times it is easier to let matters resolve themselves.

The ability to withstand pressure often depends on the level of community support for opposition. You seek reinforcement that others will view the land use proposal with the same caution. You want to know that you are on solid ground in opposing a popularly accepted development choice. If your support wanes, or if there is discord among opposition members, doubt will grow, threatening to break your focus.

Try not to let this come to pass. It is important to maintain energy and conviction throughout the opposition process, especially before public hearings. It is doubly important to maintain "flow." If your efforts lack continuity, the proponent will jump on this weakness. The opposition cannot afford to blow hot and then cold.

A proponent who is in tune with the psychology of the opposition will often attempt to disrupt its continuity. For instance, if she senses defeat she may ask for a continuation of hearings. Especially in local issues, such a request creates hardship for opponents. Expecting resolution, they are suddenly confronted with the prospect of several additional months of indecision and effort. Meanwhile, all the proponent has to do to maintain continuity is motivate her professionals, which is as easy as writing a check to pay their salaries.

But proponents shouldn't be castigated for adopting delay tactics. Delays may truly be an opportunity to achieve consensus, or perhaps to more thoroughly consider community suggestions. And in fairness, opponents frequently employ the same tactics when they sense defeat, hoping to return to the table better prepared and with more support. Of course, delaying the decision may well reshuffle the deck to the other side's advantage.

Will the opposing neighbors be available when the issue is next considered? And will they be prepared for the new information that the proponent brings to the hearing? Perhaps. If they retain their flow—their focus, energy, and enthusiasm.

As opponents, expect the unexpected when you are preparing for public meetings. Expect adversity. Expect community pressure from your friends and neighbors. Expect delay. Only by steeling yourself against these contingencies will you conquer them.

CHAPTER 14

The Importance
of Decorum

The time has arrived. A public hearing is the only way forward. The preliminaries are out of the way. As opponents, you are prepared, confident, and convinced that the offending development proposal must be fully exposed to public scrutiny. You stand ready to protect your home, business, and community from desecration.

How will you be perceived? How will your presentation be received? In both cases, you will improve your prospects if, in the heat of public battle, you respect decorum, show empathy, and avoid labels. These are the first of several meeting rules I'll be suggesting in the next few chapters.

MEETING RULE: RESPECT DECORUM.

Your first and most important task is to keep the decisionmakers' ears open. You cannot convince them of the merits of your opposition if they are not listening. And they won't listen if you don't respect decorum in the public meeting chamber. Most decisionmakers view the chamber with a certain reverence. They have worked hard to get there. They view public service as a privilege, and they consider what they do as being of great public importance. Moreover, they are acutely aware of what is occurring in the chamber when public presentations are being made. They know who's talking to whom. They know who is being courteous and who is not. They know whether the proponents and opponents respect or disdain each other, the staff, and the decisionmakers themselves. And they usually take all of this seriously.

Too many opposition groups make the most basic mistakes: they don't show a reciprocal deference. It is not unusual for an opposition group, full of nervous energy and waiting for a hearing, to conduct a public gabfest before their own time opens on the agenda. This behavior signals to decisionmakers that opponents don't find other agenda items are as important as their own, and that they don't respect or understand the process of public debate and decision making. The risk is that you may lose the attention and concern of members of the commission, council, or agency. They turn a deaf ear, even if the slight is completely unintentional. And in public battles, every vote counts.

Here are several hints for proper conduct in public chambers:

Arrive early and participate in the rituals of the meeting. Many councils or commissions start with the Pledge of Allegiance. They recognize various citizens within the community for good deeds or accomplishments. Meetings generally start on a note of good will. Your attention during these preliminaries sends a signal to decisionmakers that you are willing to be a part of the public decisionmaking process and that you have respect for it.

While other agenda items are being considered, be seated towards the back of the public chambers and allow other members of the public the opportunity to come forward with their items. This is common courtesy. Never speak or chat during public deliberations on another item. Whispering is offensive.

Opposition members and their experts should be seated together if possible. By sitting together, the opposition shows that it is united and focused. It also clearly conveys to the decisionmaking body who is part of the opposition effort.

When an agenda item is being heard, it is always a good practice for those presenting the opposition, their experts, and their leaders to be seated near the front of the public chamber. This projects confidence and allows for quick response and easy travel to the podium, making opponents more human in the minds of the decisionmakers. They need to know that their decisions affect real people, not some abstract public.

Use titles of respect and do not digress into informality no matter how well you know a particular staff member or decisionmaker. You should always refer to the chairperson as "Madam Chair, Chairman, or Mayor." Your should always refer to board members by their title, "Members of the Council, Commissioner." Always state your name and address for the record and so that decisionmakers know who you are.

Get to the point. Don't tell folksy stories or humorous anecdotes. Your sense of what is funny may not be shared by the decisionmaker, and the clock is ticking. Play it safe. Stick to the script.

After a presentation ends, take the discussion outside. Often members of the opposition dive into postmortem discussion, perhaps out of relief or, in the event of an adverse decision, frustration. Don't burn your bridges. The decisionmakers may remember exactly how you reacted to their decision, and if it was discourteously, they may not feel compelled to give you the benefit of the doubt next time you come before them. At any rate, your chat won't be appreciated.

In short, if you want decisionmakers to take you seriously, you must take them seriously too.

MEETING RULE: SHOW EMPATHY.

Next, and closely related, is empathy: that is, seeing the development proposal through the eyes of the proponent and making clear that you do when you address the decisionmakers. "Madam chair, members of the board, we understand that the proponent's position will likely be . . ." "We sympathize with this position and would ask that you accept our competing view for the following reasons." "We know that this is a difficult choice, but one which the proponent is in the best position to overcome."

Empathy keeps you in the game by retaining the decisionmaker's attention. It tells the decisionmakers that you understand the place and role of each party in the dispute. Don't grasp defeat from the jaws of victory by snickering and jeering. Take the high road, and pray that the proponent attacks like a mountain lion. What a contrast. Who will have the upper hand?

Empathy should not lessen your conviction or confidence—it should simply soften the rough edges of presentation. If you show empathy and you are fortunate enough to prevail, the result will be more acceptable to all parties, including the proponent. If the proponent loses a fair fight, he is less likely to proceed to appeals or in a direction counter to your concerns. But if he feels that he was blind-sided by a brickbat, he'll be looking for a club of his own.

An example from New Jersey illustrates how an effective show of empathy can make difficult decisions more palatable. The City of New Brunswick proposed to demolish a public housing high-rise development called New Brunswick Homes (*New Brunswick Home News and Tribune,* May 5, 8, 1996). The proposal had a tortured history. Its stated purpose was to make way for a new municipal police station and low-rise apartments. The demolition would displace over a thousand residents, an emotionally compelling consequence.

The proponent, the City of New Brunswick, was in for a fight. The opponent residents were potential victims. But each party reached an understanding of each other's needs. The city devised a plan guaranteeing alternative housing for the low-income residents. The residents recognized that the city did its best to act in their interest.

City officials recognized the reluctance of residents to travel to public chambers to hear the final plan. Wisely, they arranged to present it at a meeting hall in the project, before the media and the general public were notified. The residents recognized the extra effort. The plan is moving forward. Empathy legitimized the decision.

MEETING RULE: AVOID LABELS.

Remember the old school yard admonition: Don't call people names. Name calling will only hurt the opposition's chances of success.

It has become fashionable for proponents and the media to attach labels like "nimbys" or "enviro-nazis" to development opponents, lumping them indiscriminately as obstructionists who don't appreciate the societal values of growth and development. The labels are hot buttons pushed to encourage decisionmakers' predisposition towards growth.

In fact, for the most part opponents tend to be realists. They want development choices that are compatible with their homes and investments. Doesn't everybody? In this sense we are all nimbys.

If it's fashionable for unabashedly pro-growth forces to name call, that doesn't mean you should stoop to the same level. Don't call the proponent a "developer," "bully," or "cookie cutter." Don't place yourself on the defensive unnecessarily. Public labeling will backfire.

The same rule applies to decisionmakers and staff. It is always amazing to watch a citizen yell "Liar!" or "Thief!" to a decisionmaker, or accuse him of being bought off by a proponent. Is the decisionmaker expected to keep a level head several minutes or hours later when she is voting on the development proposal?

Land use battles are highly emotional. There are proponents who do not respect the environment. There are proponents who believe that their business is the most important in the world, even if it destroys others. There are proponents who believe that as long as their buildings have open views, they should be able to destroy someone else's. In their minds, they are just smarter than everybody.

Don't ever let their insensitivity goad you into name calling. Nothing will close the ears of decisionmakers faster than a name calling contest. If you want a fair hearing, keep a lid on it.

Let's consider the use of the preceding meeting rules in the case of the Billie family, part of the Independent Traditional Seminole Nation. This thirty-member Seminole tribe lives on a small patch of land in rural Collier County, Florida, which, though it is located in the Everglades, is not technically on the reservation. The Seminoles live in chickee huts made of palm fronds, grasses, and mud walls. Several of the huts have been outfitted with electricity and plumbing, arguably not in strict conformance with county building and electrical codes. The Seminoles refer to their collection of chickee homes as a village.

They have lived in such structures for years without government interference. Then in mid-1995 code enforcement officials, alerted by a fire call, conducted an informal inspection of the village and issued citations for noncompliance with building codes and zoning requirements. The village members did not accept the authority of the county to apply its ordinances. Conversely, the county believed that it had a responsibility to apply its codes uniformly for the safety of all residents.

The struggle attracted the attention of the national media. The Billie family made several impressive showings at public meetings to advance their cause, which was to protect their traditional way of life. Over three days in May 1996, they marched forty miles from their village to the Collier County Courthouse, where they waited to address the Collier County Board of Commissioners. At a public meeting on May 14, 1996, their sixty or more supporters, including Native Americans from Canada, South America, and different parts of the United States, many clothed in ceremonial dress and holding protest signs, sat quietly through a long list of prior agenda items. Their spokesperson, Danny Billie, stood quietly near the podium with his prayer staff for over four hours.

When it came time to speak, various members of the group made presentations to the county board, charging insensitivity on its part. Several presentations tied the county's actions to global oppression of indigenous races. One speaker rashly accused the board of genocide. Native Americans from all over the Americas recounted long stories about the plight of disappearing Indian cultures.

There were chants and loud whoops of support in the normally ordered public chamber. There were songs and flute playing. At the end of the presentation, all the Independent Traditional Seminoles and their supporters, men, women, and children, spontaneously approached the dais and shook hands with each of the commissioners one by one. Then they quietly filed out of the chambers to the halls outside, where the reporters and television cameras were waiting.

The Independent Traditional Seminoles were only partly successful in showing empathy. By assigning guilt to the decisionmakers for the historical actions of their ancestors, the speakers were being indiscriminate. Obviously, the county board had not practiced genocide. But their show of respect through the closing ritual of greeting and thanks perhaps softened their words by demonstrating that the statements were not personal, but rather represented deeply held convictions about a modern culture that they reject and that threatens their way of life.

If the litmus test is whether the village members *elicited* empathy, then they succeeded—most television viewers were touched by their plight. But no doubt their confrontational technique put some distance between the Seminoles and the decisionmakers themselves.

The presentation was a study in contrasts, all advanced by one opposition group. Nonetheless, it was effective. The county and the village members ultimately settled their differences in a way sensitive to both. The village was designated a cultural facility, allowing for latitude in the siting of buildings, and county inspectors were allowed inspections on basic building code issues.

In public meetings respect received is respect earned, by following decorum, showing empathy, and demonstrating courtesy. These most basic meeting rules are fundamental to opposition success.

MEETING RULE: STAY FIT.

There is a lot more to decorum than minding your manners and striving to understand the proponent. Appearance counts too.

If you are well dressed and physically fit, it will tell the decisionmakers a great deal about how you perceive your role and how serious you are as an opponent.

Suppose that your land use conflict involves the construction of a mega mall, destruction of habitat, or senseless laying of more roads. The issue is charged with emotion. Proponents and opponents have spent months publicly slugging it out. Newspaper articles have been written. Talk shows have sensationalized the debate. Opponents have spent more time away from friends, family, and jobs than they ever could have imagined at the inception of the battle—that first glance at a newspaper article or call from a neighbor announcing the proposal. They're tired, and they long to return to a normal life.

Proponents have spent more money and time than they anticipated. Economically, there is no turning back. Decisionmakers have been lobbied ad nauseam. They are weary. The late night phone calls are getting downright obnoxious. But their political future is at stake; they want to do the right thing.

All sides are sleep deprived. Some prepared through the night before the meeting. Others could not get to sleep the night before. Still others had to work all day before attending this night's meeting. And many are hungry. They didn't get a chance to eat dinner in their rush. In small group meetings before the public forum, everybody tanks up with coffee. Everyone is wired.

All parties arrive with their experts, performing rituals of intimidation directed at unsettling the other parties and convincing themselves of the correctness of their position. The effort of intimidation ratchets the emotional levels another notch above the red line, just to ensure that all involved parties feel maximum pressure and are disposed to battle.

The public meeting gets under way, but takes unpredictable turns. Routine matters on the agenda that precede the land use debate are taking much longer than expected. The meeting drags on. The temperature rises. The chamber's ventilation and air conditioning systems are clearly not designed for the unexpected influx. Everyone is uncomfortable. They pace. They sit. They pace some more.

The decisionmakers, sensing that time is short, skip planned breaks. They need to be some place else. One of them hoped against hope that the meeting would be abbreviated. Finally, the land use debate begins. Weary, anxious minds are now going to argue and decide a matter that will define the landscape for the next hundred years.

Sound familiar, in whole or in part? It might be exaggerated, but every land use conflict contains some element of this scenario.

The people who argue and decide land use cases should be attentive, like doctors who perform surgery. Public meetings are physically demanding. Those who are fit will be the most alert and will have a leg up on their adversaries.

The Marathon

The week before the meeting, then, make sure you get plenty of exercise and sleep. Eat well and try to avoid stressful situations. Directly before the meeting, skip the coffee. No doubt your nervous system will be active enough without the added jolt of fifty milligrams of caffeine. Try drinking water instead—it carries oxygen to the brain.

Treat preparation for public hearings no less seriously than preparation for those other experiences in your life which are equally important. You don't have to be a health nut. But do be aware of the physical rigors of the public hearing arena. Place yourself in a position to send your message most effectively.

MEETING RULE: DRESS YOUR PART.

A corollary to maintaining your health is maintaining your appearance. Appearance is a subtle factor in public decisionmaking. It tells the decisionmaker how you feel about yourself, and implicitly, your position.

Of course, there is no one acceptable manner of dress in public chambers. Public meetings accommodate many different roles, and each participant should dress to fit his or hers. Professional consultants should probably opt for formality, which shows respect to decisionmakers. But the sea captain, marina owner, shrimper, farmer, or mountaineer should not feel compelled to wear a three-piece suit. The best guideline is to dress neatly but comfortably. Don't dress up or down. Be yourself. Play your role. For that will give you the most confidence as you seek to articulate your case.

Fitness and appearance are an integral part of decorum, and decorum is an integral part of success.

CHAPTER 15

Understanding the Decisionmakers

O *ne* of my former law partners, a litigator, followed a philosophy of jury selection that he referred to as *twelve warm bodies*. He would dispense with lengthy selection procedures, eliminating only prospective jurors with an obvious prejudice, and play to the jury as drawn. In land use battles, opponents are stuck with twelve warm bodies, prejudices and all. What you see is what you get. You are bound to their life philosophies, political views, spousal influence, community ties, and all their strengths and weaknesses.

MEETING RULE:
UNDERSTAND THE DECISIONMAKERS.

This is critical. It is an ominous sign when a citizen comes before a decisionmaking body and doesn't even know the names of its members. As opponents, you must play to your audience. If your audience speaks one language and you speak another, you've wasted your time because the audience won't understand you.

Below is a list, not exhaustive, of the sort of questions you should answer.

1. What are the names of the decisionmakers?

2. Where will each one be sitting at the public meeting?

3. Are they elected or appointed? If elected, do they represent certain districts within the community? For instance, are they representatives from single-member districts? Were they elected on certain campaign issues or promises? Were they elected with the support of certain groups, and if so, who were they? If the decisionmakers are appointed, who appointed them and why?

4. What is the political background of each decisionmaker? What boards, bodies, or other positions did each hold before being elected or appointed?

5. What are their occupational backgrounds and talents? Do their skills relate to the development proposal?

6. What are their individual voting records on similar proposals?

7. What are the political alliances on the board? Whom do individual members tend to vote with and be influenced by?

There are as many different decisionmakers as there are shapes of snow flakes. Here are just a few types you may encounter:

The Position Thinker

Position thinkers have their minds made up before a matter comes to a vote. They lock in like heat-seeking missiles once they decide which way to go. For the position thinker, being 51 percent sure is the same as being 99 percent sure.

Position thinkers take all the guesswork out of the process. They announce to the world on radio and in the newspaper which way they are going to vote before they even arrive at the hearing. Their weakness is that because they commit so early, when new information surfaces, which it inevitably will, they are so far out on a limb that a graceful retreat is difficult.

The Authoritarian

Related to the position thinker is the authoritarian. The authoritarian recognizes that the municipality is the boss and will almost always vote in support of staff and its position. The authoritarian rarely questions the advice of staff experts. He forgets that experts are merely facilitators and that he is the policymaker. The authoritarian is at least predictable and with a solid staff can be an asset to the decisionmaking process. However, he has little tolerance for creative arguments or complex discussion. In the authoritarian's world there is a right way and a wrong way with no shades of gray.

The Self-Promoter

The self-promoter has a personal political agenda. The self promoter views all proposals through the lenses of that agenda. She tends to form political alliances with certain board members, who vote as a block.

The self-promoter follows the politically expedient course. Facts are often secondary. Many self-promoters are unable to grasp complex planning, zoning, or scientific issues. You will win or lose depending on whether your goals are consistent with the self-promoter's political agenda. The most dangerous self-promoter is the lawyer, accountant, engineer, or other professional who imposes her occupational view on the rest of the decisionmaking body as a substitute for the advice of staff.

The Constituency Voter

Constituency voters want to know which way the political wind is blowing. They view their role as executing the public will of the moment. An opinion poll on the issue at hand would reveal the vote of the constituency voter. Constituency voters know how they got elected and are loyal to their supporters regardless of whether, privately, they might sympathize with the views of others.

142

The Ceremonial Voter

The ceremonial voter revels in the prestige of public office. The ceremonial voter always takes the path of least resistance and is extremely deferential to his staff. It is the staff's job to make him look good and protect him from public acrimony. In the eyes of ceremonial voters, staff members are the experts. To them he abrogates not only questions of fact, but decisions of policy as well. It is especially dangerous when the municipal attorney takes an active political role. It is like having an extra member of the decisionmaking body to contend with. In essence, the attorney has a vote even though she is not elected.

The Independent Thinker

Independent thinkers listen and analyze. They make their own decisions, often from scratch. They challenge assumptions and they challenge advice. They want to make sure that each decision is being well thought through. They will take the time to make informed decisions, often frustrating their fellow decisionmakers. They do not commit to positions in advance of meetings, and they tend to be judicious in their decisionmaking.

Independent thinkers are willing to be on the short end of a minority vote. They do not view themselves as running in a popularity contest. For them, politics is not usually a career and they tend to be quite talented outside the political arena. Independent thinkers often rely on the feedback of those closest to them. Family and close friends play an important role in the decisionmaking of the independent thinker.

Braveheart

Braveheart is a cousin of the independent thinker. Braveheart is a kamikaze fighter who harbors a strong suspicion of government, which is probably why he was elected. Braveheart challenges every proposal and every decision at every turn. He is the staff members' nightmare, because he makes them accountable. They may try to isolate braveheart from the other decisionmakers. Braveheart is always searching for the state-of-the-art solution and believes that there is undoubtedly a better way of doing everything. No issue is too small for his scrutiny.

Braveheart is like a third party sitting on the decisionmaking body. Precisely because of his isolation, his is often a swing vote between otherwise evenly divided historical alliances. Braveheart doesn't align with other decisionmakers regularly.

As opponents, it will help you immensely if you understand the makeup of the decisionmaking body with respect to your particular land use challenge. The chemistry of that body might well frame your strategy.

People make decisions in different ways. To communicate your position, you should establish some common ground with each of the decisionmakers, as much of a challenge as that might be. Frame your argument in terms that they may relate to.

MEETING RULE: COUNT NOSES.

At the end of the day, after all the lobbying, public flagellation, expert shoot-outs, eloquent and not so eloquent speech making, obligatory chest thumping, and teeth gnashing, public decisions arrive at one question: Who has the votes? Though opponents may have taken great pains to understand the makeup of the decisionmaking body, they had better be able to count.

Too often, this meeting rule is lost in the fog of rhetoric and process. It means more than knowing the predisposition of individual decisionmakers on a given class of issue. It means knowing exactly where they stand on the specific land use issue.

We would like to believe that decisionmakers provide all interested parties with the opportunity to make their case before publicly announcing how they intend to vote. Frequently, however, decisionmakers feel compelled to do a straw vote before arguments have been completely aired. Well in advance of the hearing, then, opponents need to understand the likely views of each decisionmaker on the land use issue. Like racing sailors, they must be able to read the first furrow of the jib.

Because there is a common predisposition toward the early decision, lobbying is sometimes unavoidable. By lobbying, I'm not referring to the sophisticated art practiced in Washington. There over fifteen thousand lobbyists make it their business to know how members of the House and Senate are disposed to vote on a given issue. And they do it for a living. Fortunately, land use decisions that affect your home, business, and community are usually decided at the local level. In local venues, decisionmakers have a stronger interest in maintaining a perception of fairness than decisionmakers in Washington. This is true for two reasons. First, local news is the news that counts to most citizens. And second, in local communities people have to live with each other after the decision is made. In a sense, local decisionmakers are more directly accountable for their actions.

Though a number of manuals deliver precise formulas for lobbying proponents before public meetings, in truth there is no one perfect method. As we've seen, local decisionmaking is an uncertain process at best. But there are some steps you can take that will help level the playing field between you and the proponent: sending notice letters, feeling out decisionmakers for their positions, lobbying if necessary, preventing premature straw polls that solidify positions, and counting noses to the very end.

Start counting noses by sending a notice letter. We've already discussed this. Make sure the decisionmakers know that you are out there. The notice letter need not state opposition, only that you are studying the proposal and trying to learn more about it. This letter keeps everyone honest, and may give the decisionmaker some pause before formulating positions too quickly.

Next, feel decisionmakers out for their positions on issues related to the one under consideration. Is the proposal so similar to other issues that the decisionmaker has voted on that he will surely vote the same way? For instance, does the proposal involve locating a business in a redevelopment area, and does the decisionmaker view all development within the area as good or appropriate development? Or was the decisionmaker elected on a platform of preserving neighborhoods, so that any commercial development is considered undesirable? More important is to feel decisionmakers out on the specific development proposal.

Has the proponent already lobbied the decisionmakers? Has a particular one become an advocate for the proponent? You can go down the list one by one and ask the decisionmakers directly, or listen to radio talk shows or public meeting presentations.

This strategy might help. Well before the meeting, you might ask the decisionmakers this leading question: "What additional information do you feel you need to make a decision when the time comes?" A follow up: "What information if any would make you vote against the development proposal, or to approve it with conditions?"

The answers to these questions will be telling. Are the decisionmakers being reasonable and objective, or are they making demands designed to camouflage a decision already made?

The next step in the process of counting noses is deciding how much and whether to lobby. The prevailing wisdom in most neighborhood and civic organizations is to lobby hard and often, recreating in microcosm the sort of Washington intrigue that, ironically, we rail against daily.

Power lobbying on a local level lends itself to the strategies of turn up the volume, constrained chaos, and pure political heat. Often power lobbying works,

QUASI-JUDICIAL HEARINGS

Snyder v. Board of County Commissioners of Brevard County is one of the leading cases in the country on what constitutes a quasi-judicial proceeding. This 1992 Florida supreme court case prohibited individuals from lobbying local officials on petitions for zoning changes affecting specific parcels, conditional uses, and variances. This rule was later modified by the Florida legislature in a statute which allows local governments to adopt ordinances allowing lobbying so long as the lobbying is disclosed in the public hearing and the opponents have an opportunity to respond.

momentarily. It gives decisionmakers pause when there is a mass uprising against a development proposal, though they may do no more than scramble for a strategy to placate their constituents or profess openmindedness while watching the development proposal travel to approval, the result they actually favor.

This isn't the only reason power lobbying has its limitations. Decisionmakers don't enjoy being pushed around. If highly pressured, they may respond out of pure frustration rather than thoughtful reflection.

There is also compelling legal reason to approach individual lobbying cautiously. Certain zoning and planning decisions may be considered quasi-judicial, depending on the law of your state. In this case, the law may consider decisionmakers to be like judges, who are presumably impartial before announcing an actual decision. As it is inappropriate to speak with a judge prior to decision, it may be inappropriate to influence decisionmakers in the same way. In states that recognize the quasi-judicial nature of certain proceedings, proponents have a right to decisions based on factual records, not on the record of citizen commentary.

Regardless of the technical requirements of local law, community mores may dictate that unrestrained lobbying is inappropriate. As a strategy, it may backfire. In this case you might want to adopt a straightforward factual approach. Outlearn the staff. Outprepare the proponent. Draw on outside resources that challenge the local state of the art and move the frontier of local development to a higher level. Instead of lobbying, educate.

I am not suggesting that opposition should be naïve. If a proponent has presented the staff and decisionmakers with one wildly skewed side of the story in an effort to "wire" a vote and discredit possible opposition in advance, then you may have no choice but to engage decisionmakers and begin the slow process of scraping disinformation off the walls. But this should be done in a focused and educational way.

One answer might be to invite decisionmakers to a group meeting, where they will discover the depth of opposition. First on the guest list should be the decisionmaker whom you suspect of being most unfriendly to the opposition, for it is that person who needs the most convincing. Next, invite the independent thinkers who have open minds and a propensity to listen. You may only be able to moderate decisionmakers' views. But moderation is not always a loss.

Group lobbying tends to be most acceptable to decisionmakers because it emulates the openness of a public meeting. They are able to gauge how a community or neighborhood feels rather than a select few citizens.

What if lobbying is a moot issue because the result of an upcoming vote is already public knowledge? It is disheartening when the local paper publishes its straw poll as a headline story before the public hearing and predicts the outcome. It is equally disappointing when decisionmakers accept motions and seconds before listening to public input. Such actions nullify the public process. However, well intended decisionmakers who try to expedite the hearing process by letting all involved know where they stand may send a message that what takes place outside the public chamber is more important than what happens within it.

In this case, cry foul. If the offending party is the local newspaper, confront it. The newspaper is supposed to be the voice of intellectual honesty. If the offending party is the decisionmaker let her know that you expect a fair hearing. Use the situation to your advantage. You may actually force decisionmakers to be more reflective.

Of course, even if the outcome isn't cast in concrete, decisionmakers usually communicate their leanings. Their questions signal their thoughts and concerns. In your presentation, focus on those questions that appear critical to the decisionmakers. Don't be so married to a particular emphasis that you fail to respond to what is really important—influencing votes.

Often decisionmakers will not commit to a position but will probe themselves. They will want to know if opponents will accept compromises. Be ready with your answers. It is critical to know who accepts and who rejects your position if you are to answer questions directed towards compromise. And that means counting noses—during the public hearing as well as before it.

CHAPTER 16

The Strategy of Presentation

The public meeting is like a painting of Paul Klee where viewers, for our purposes decisionmakers, must draw ordered conclusions and meaning from a canvas of chaos. As an opponent, to achieve ordered conclusions in public meeting environments you must advocate decisions grounded in logic presented in an understandable and effective way. This leads us to the next meeting rule.

MEETING RULE: BE STRATEGIC IN PRESENTING THE OPPOSITION'S POSITION.

Take the high road and fight a battle of intellect with sincerity. Decisionmakers and proponents of incompatible development steel themselves against the force of high-volume public opinion. Citizens groups that merely show up to say "We don't like that" are doomed to failure.

Why don't you like that? What specifically is wrong with the proposal? Where is the failure of logic? What competing value should prevail over that being proposed? What is your authority, and why is it more credible than that of the proponents?

Decisionmakers are used to hearing complaints about growth and its impacts. They tend to view them as the whining of children on the playground. Their response to vague complaints is that growth is inevitable. As opponents, you can only overcome this fatalistic attitude with factual, philosophical alternatives.

A dramatic example is playing itself out in Salt Lake County, Utah, an area with one of the highest growth rates in the country. As reported by the *Desert News* (April 21, 1996), the southwest part of the county has been a last frontier not only of unspoiled nature but also of resistance to planning and zoning enforcement. But the pressures of urbanization and the stark potential of unregulated development have rendered this traditional attitude dangerous. Growth, especially unregulated, is not a fait accompli. The residents have begun taking control of their destiny by focusing their discussion, on the inadequacy of roads and water resources. Will their decisions made by the residents of Salt Lake County withstand the test of time? When the children of today look back in the year 2020, will they see a string of postage stamp subdivisions relying on a rural road system and facing chronic water shortages? Or will they see contextual development characterized by open space and preservation of the natural environment?

How the issues are conceptualized and presented today will make the ultimate difference in this land use drama. If the public discussion is nothing but a series of objections with no articulation of philosophy, prospects are bleak. If the objection is "there is no water" then developers will engineer a method of creating water supplies and distribution systems. If the objection is "there are no roads" then developers will adopt impact fees to ensure that roads are built. But if the discussion centers on broader philosophies and development challenges, starting with the most basic question of what level of growth is acceptable, then there is room for hope. What planning decisions will accommodate an acceptable level of growth? What planning decisions will accommodate a community value of open space preservation? What planning decisions will minimize the public burden of infrastructure development so that the bill doesn't fall due to taxpayers in the future?

If the residents allow proponent developers to remove short-term objections without addressing the long-term philosophical questions of how much growth is acceptable, they will move into the future by chance rather than design. This is true for all communities.

Having command of the substantive arguments, you must also have command of meeting dynamics, one of the most important of which is knowing how to use time effectively.

MEETING RULE: MANAGE THE CLOCK.

At a public meeting the clock can be your friend or your enemy. Using the clock to your advantage takes anticipation, skill, and a fair amount of good luck.

Many opponents naïvely prepare their argument without asking whether it can be presented within the likely period of time allotted by decisionmakers. They cannot imagine that decisionmakers won't allot at least as much time as the proponent receives.

As slow as public hearings may seem, once you are on the stage, time flies! Before the meeting, consider how much time you'll need, and how much you're likely to have. Is there anything that might curb the amount of time you're allowed? There are certain common mistakes opponents make when it comes to the clock.

Poor Logistics

As opponents, you won't have the luxury of much time to make your presentation. And every moment spent tacking blue line drawings on presentation boards that no one can see, or fiddling with slide projectors, overheads, and extension cords, is time not spent in presentation. It takes away from something else, perhaps an important point. Know the layout of the room. Be prepared and set up ahead of time. Be ready to present when your number is called.

Not Requesting Equal Time

The proponent will attempt to take the lion's share of available time. Not until after she has made her case in favor of the development proposal will the public and opposition be asked to participate. This is like the children's game of keep away: If you don't have the ball, you cannot make your points.

Decisionmakers are tired by the time it's the opposition's turn. Perhaps they have followed the proponent's logic and have already made up their mind. At this point, opponents are definitely swimming upstream.

The remedy for keep away is to try and establish an even playing field by setting the procedural rules in advance of the public meeting. Notify the chairperson or staff manager that you intend to speak, perhaps with a group, and that you request the same amount of time as the proponent.

Allowing the Hour Glass to Run Out

Perhaps for reasons unrelated to the proponent, time is short. Prior agenda items were lengthy. The hour is late. Some decisionmaker has an engagement. When you are in opposition, time is almost always short.

The remedy for the empty hourglass is to plan for it in advance. Approach the meeting with adaptable scripts. Have a short version prepared that makes the key points verbally and visually and puts minor points in writing for the record. Make sure your key speakers get up to bat.

Let the chairperson know the outline of your script when you make your presentation. Then follow the script.

Do your best to keep the presentation interesting and to the point. In land use debates people have a pernicious habit of circling around the point, like people at a mall who drive for twenty minutes to find a spot a few feet closer.

Decisionmakers are more inclined to listen to presentations that are brief, nonrepetitive, and interesting.

Being Pushed into the Hurry Up Offense

It may be the decisionmakers rather than the proponents who push opponents into the hurry up offense. If you play a methodical game of set plays, don't try to become the master of the fast break.

Commissions and councils often adopt procedural rules that limit the time public speakers have to make their case. Usually, the chairperson of the decision-making body has discretion in how such rules are applied. For instance, she might allot more time to the citizen who is most substantially affected by the proposal, or who is the best prepared. Opponent experts who show up to counter the proponent's expert testimony may occasionally be limited or cut off because the chairperson's mind is made up or because it is her responsibility to move the meeting forward.

DUE PROCESS COMES IN DIFFERENT FORMS

We are all used to hearing about the taking of property without just compensation. This is called a denial of substantive due process. However, inherent in the Fifth and Fourteenth Amendments to the U.S. Constitution is the right to be heard—procedural due process. Hearing rules are grounded in procedural due process. This means that as opponents, where you have a substantial interest in the outcome of the proceeding, you have a right to be fairly heard and meeting rules must accommodate that right.

If there were no such rules, some public meetings would come to a grinding halt. However, keeping a level playing field is very important. Proponents often spend hours in preparation and presentation. Affording citizens who will be substantially affected by a proposal the full opportunity to be heard is only fair. To deprive them of that opportunity in the interest of abbreviated meetings is a denial of fundamental due process.

In trying to accommodate decisionmakers, do not be bullied into a position

154

where you are not allowed to develop your arguments. If the chairperson curbs your time to the detriment of your argument, make sure it is in writing and included in the record.

Prolonging the Meeting

Not uncommonly, decisionmakers signal their predisposition to decide in favor of the opposition, but the opposition nonetheless maintains a filibuster. This may upset the decisionmakers, causing them to re-assess their positions. Determine whether you really want them to think longer about where they stand. It behooves you to read the tea leaves.

Presenting Out of Order

Certain opponents should make certain points at certain times in a public meeting. Opponents have many perspectives. Adopt a strategy that best displays all perspectives in the argument. One person's point, which you may have thought was obscure earlier, might establish common ground with a decisionmaker and thereby sway the vote in your favor. Think through how points relate to each other and how they are going to be made. You might have a coordinator make sure that each speaker presents his or her argument at the proper time.

Start the meeting with the understanding that your opportunity for presentation will be limited. Try to gauge how much time you will have. What is the mood of the decisionmakers? Are they pressed for time? What are the other items on the agenda? How long are they likely to take? Above all, it is important to remain flexible. If you are able to adapt to changing conditions, you improve the chances of success.

Public presentation is an art. You are on stage, and now everything you have to say must come together in a limited time. Having developed the substance and an awareness of the need for time management, you are ready to consider some additional pointers for making effective public presentations.

These have all been mentioned by now. This is a reminder:

Break your presentation down into three segments: professional presentation, public presentation, and a summary or request for relief. What do you want? Then fluidly move between each.

Orchestrate the presentation with a common theme. Why won't the development proposal withstand the test of time? What is not being said that the decisionmakers should consider? Be concrete. Do not speculate.

Briefly summarize the opposition script so that there are no surprises for either decisionmakers or opponents in allotting time.

Do not be any more legalistic than necessary. A legalistic approach will devour valuable time. On legal matters, decisionmakers will virtually always follow the advice of the municipal attorney. If there are legal arguments to be made, they should generally be made in advance of the public hearing. If possible, highlight that the development proposal does not meet the zoning criteria that the decisionmakers are bound to follow. When there are no written criteria for development applica*tions, focus on policy.*

Emphasize the economics of what is being lost. Do not rest your opposition on the bald assertion that there are "thousands of dollars going down the drain." Exactly what is being lost? How much property value and tax revenue are being placed at risk? What public cost is inherent in allowing the development proposal to proceed? Is there additional cost associated with new schools and public infrastructure such as roads, sewer, and water? Is the public losing a resource that has an economic value, and what might that economic value be? If the proponent is wrong, what will it cost the public to correct his mistakes? What is the societal cost in allowing desecration of limited public resources, beaches, air and water, and wildlife habitat? These items are all capable of quantification. Developers never quantify or incorporate the external costs of development. But there are econometric models which do, and they are at least equally viable. Find them and use them.

Place a human face on the impact of the development proposal. Who will be affected? Is it acceptable that the residents of Alpena, Michigan, bear the cost and risk associated with a toxic waste-burning cement kiln near their municipal water supply and vital wetlands, where the effects are unknown but perhaps dramatic? (Envirobiz News Daily, http://www.envirobiz.com//newsdaily; December 6, 1995)

Never read your presentation. It's boring and makes you look less than sincere. Use reminder notes if necessary. Likewise, keep eye contact with the decisionmakers. Speaking to them directly displays your conviction and sincerity. A related point: don't bring along beepers or cellular phones, which have a bad habit of erupting at just the wrong time. One small beep tells decisionmakers that something else is more important than the matter at hand.

Use visuals carefully. Some decisionmakers think verbally. Some think visually. Visuals such as slides, overheads, and videos may hold the promise of added interest, especially where they overcome a proponent's blue line drawings. If visuals help decisionmakers see the development choice more vividly, use them. Make sure that any equipment you use is well tested. You can't afford to test decisionmakers' patience with a slide projector or a video screen that doesn't work. This will let them know that you are listening.

Feel the decisionmakers out. Identify their concerns and respond to them.

Spare the humor and folksy stories. Public hearings are serious business. Though one decisionmaker may find you personable, another may consider you disrespectful or just plain annoying.

Never lose your cool, even when baited. If you respond emotionally, expect emotion in return. You set the standard. And never pick a fight with a decisionmaker unnecessarily. Belligerence only detracts from your message, and it won't win you sympathy from the other decisionmakers.

Don't ever publicly embarrass anyone needlessly, not even the proponent. They will remember. Next time it could be you on the short end.

You may cry foul if appropriate. But do so on the basis of fact, not supposition.

Most land use proposals travel through several hearings. If an approach doesn't work in a meeting of a planning board or commission, don't repeat the same mistake before decisionmakers charged with making the final decision. Use what you learn as a chance to improve.

Be consistent. Inconsistency damages your credibility.

A hypothetical example: Assume that a local church proposes the construction of a forty-thousand-square-foot facility in a neighborhood that has one two-lane local road, not a major collector. All of the neighborhood is developed except for the ten-acre parcel on which the church is to be constructed. The local road is the primary means by which the residents of the neighborhood enter and exit the community.

The church is a sympathetic proponent. Many of its parishioners are community leaders. The church has chosen the site because of the comparatively low cost of the land. With its prominence in the community the church leadership has a zoning approval clearly in its sights, but it has been a little slow to examine the effect of the facility on the neighborhood. The church members are on a mission of their own, spiritual development, which is paramount to any possible neighborhood concerns. In their eyes the neighbors ought to view the facility with the same enthusiasm.

Because of high peak-hour traffic volume, and in order to provide adequate parking, the church will have to pave the ten acres, lot line to lot line. Use of the church is designated as a conditional use in a residential zone.

You and your neighbors are concerned. Opposition might tear the community apart. You know many of the church leaders. Still, the church facility could dramatically alter the character of the community. How do you proceed in a public meeting? You can hardly begin by saying: "I mean no ill will towards the church, but I just don't like the idea. Think of the traffic coming into our nice quiet neighborhood. And it will destroy our property values. My family and I have lived in our home all of our life and the church coming in just is not right." Nice try, but you probably lose. For every emotional argument that you have the church will have an equally compelling argument.

Try this instead:

Churches can be good neighbors, I understand that. And there are many locations within our community where churches have in fact served as good neighbors. The potential problems I see with this proposal are as follows:

1. The trip generation for the church services is equal to X under the municipal code; however, the national standard, described in the American Society of Transportation Engineers Trip Generation Manual, is equal to Y. As a community we want this church to be successful, we want it to do as well as or better than churches in other communities. But for much of Sunday and on church holidays my family and emergency vehicles may not be able to safely enter the neighborhood because of the additional traffic burden.

2. The site is too small. There is no capacity for on-street parking, and all overflow parking will be forced onto the neighbors' lawns.

3. The site has an alternative use that is more compatible with our residential zoning, and that might give the property a higher value without affecting that of the neighbors.

4. The access road is a local road with narrow lanes, and there is no available right-of-way for widening the road. Even if the road could be widened, the extra land would have to come from neighbors' front yards, which would change the complexion of the neighborhood.

5. There are X number of properly zoned alternative sites that could accommodate the facility better, and where it would be more compatible with its surroundings.

6. Before we allow this decision as a community, let's review the alternative locations and their availability. Which is the winning argument?

Having used this particular example, I should add that churches can be good neighbors. They frequently provide services such as daycare and space for community meetings. Churches also tend to heighten neighborhood security. A negotiated site plan for a church might be better than an un-negotiated residential development. Don't lose by winning!

CHAPTER 17

The Decision and Beyond

Arriving at a decision is like Dorothy's journey in Oz—the road is full of promise and adversity, friends and foes. And at the end of the road there may well be an unexpected outcome.

Decisionmaking in the public forum is much different than in other venues of American life. It is decision by committee. And decisions by committee tend to be confused. The challenge for opponents of a land development proposal is to make sure that the decision is logical and easily understood.

MEETING RULE: DRIVE DECISIONS.

Occasionally, a decision will be a simple yes or no. More often it will be filled with qualifying conditions: "maybes," "what ifs," "only when," "subject to," "upon completion," and a variety of others. It is your job to make sure that the final decision, for or against the opposition, reflects your efforts. See that decisionmakers address all the issues raised, and that even if adverse, the decision incorporates any qualifications that would make the development less intrusive. Having run the race, lean through the tape.

How is this done? First, keep in mind that the point of decision is as important as the hearing that precedes it. Many opposition groups develop elaborate presentations without preparing for the time when public presentations come to an end and the decisionmakers are on their own. Do they have the guidance necessary to nudge them in the direction of the opposition? They have a staff report before them. They have the proponent's written materials and request for approval. But do they have the opposition's written concerns, in clear, bulleted lists, supported by fact and accompanied by proposed alternatives or stipulations? For instance, might a decision on a golf course development be conditioned upon maintaining green space, preserving habitat, conserving water, or limiting fertilization? Or might the approval of a conditional use be subject to a limitation on hours of operation?

Perhaps you view the drafting function as the province of staff and decisionmakers, believing that you have fulfilled your responsibility by taking the time to prepare and present a position. This omission can be deadly. After the swirl of protracted public debates, some decisionmakers may simply resort to what is in front of them—their staff reports and the proponent's materials. Without your materials, their reasoning will be skewed.

What if, as opponents, you've adopted a strategy of just say no? In this case you may not want to suggest stipulations, for that would indicate a willingness to compromise. It's probably best to submit written stipulations just in case. In the heat of battle, when it is apparent that "just say no" is a less likely outcome than an unqualified yes, you may ask that the stipulations be incorporated in the decision without otherwise compromising your position. If the yes decision prevails, at least all will not be lost.

Prepared with written materials, you are ready to turn your attention to the dynamics of decisionmaking. Before the public hearing is closed, spring into action by summarizing your points and asking that they be included in any motion that is ultimately made. After the public hearing ends, it is time for motions. The decisionmaker who initiates the motion for or against the development proposal becomes the most powerful person in the chamber.

The motion maker frames the question that will be voted upon, thereby shaping the ultimate decision.

What types of motions might one expect, and what last-second suggestion might the opponents make which would nudge an outcome in the opponent's direction? Consider these:

THE QUICK KILL AND THE SLAM DUNK

These motions display the decisionmaker's penchant for a quick and final decision. The quick kill is a flat out no to the development proposal. The slam dunk is a flat out yes. Either motion is usually motivated by time pressure, and an unwillingness to listen to competing views held by other decisionmakers. Decisionmakers perform a great disservice to the public when they make such precipitous motions. It may be that they have some prearranged "deal." Or perhaps they simply have no patience and the matter is unimportant to them.

The party on the short end of the quick kill or slam dunk will feel deprived of a full and fair hearing and be more likely to seek one through litigation. There are few last-minute suggestions which can prevent these motions.

THE RELUCTANT MOTION

This motion slowly surfaces in a vacuum. None of the decisionmakers wants to handle the hot potato represented by the proposed development. Eventually, after much hemming and hawing, and many long pauses, a brave soul makes a motion with less than full confidence.

Usually, the reluctant motion is made in one of two situations: decisionmakers do not have enough information to evaluate competing alternatives, or they're relying on political winds without a wind sock.

With a reluctant motion on the horizon, the opposition should consider suggesting that the parties take more time to develop information that will change a halfhearted "yes" or "no" into a vote made with conviction.

THE MOTION OF DESPERATION

This ill-considered motion is designed to put the proponent or the opponent out of misery. It aims to prevent the protracted acrimony inherent in the public decisionmaking process. The motion isn't made with conviction. It is made for the single purpose of reaching a decision. The reasons for the decision are secondary.

As with the reluctant motion, decisionmakers should be urged to take a deep breath. A break. To come back another day. Public decisions are far too important to be made in desperation. At another time, there may be a climate more favorable to reasoned decisionmaking. The decisionmakers will have the benefit of reflection.

THE MOTION OF BEWILDERMENT

This results from information overload. The decisionmaker doesn't comprehend the proposal or the opponents' position. The motion of bewilderment leaves proponents and opponents alike shaking their heads in disbelief and wondering if they attended the same proceeding as the decisionmakers. The motion of bewilderment ignores facts, logic, and compelling professional advice. You know that a motion of bewilderment is on the table when a proponent starts to argue against it because it is so devoid of legal logic that it couldn't possibly withstand a litigation challenge.

There are only three remedies for a motion of bewilderment. First, pursue the remaining decisionmakers in the hope that more informed intellects will prevail. Second, if the motion of bewilderment becomes a decision, file a motion for reconsideration or third, head for the courts.

THE RAPIDFIRE MOTION

This common motion is made by the decisionmaker who adheres to one basic premise or set of recommendations and transforms it into a decision. Often, the rapidfire motion incorporates the recommendations of staff or other advisory bodies without modification.

The rapidfire motion is slightly more legitimate than the quick kill or the slam dunk because it is at least based on facts and reasoning, no matter how flawed. Your written position is the only strategy with a chance of staving off this motion.

Rapid Fire

THE GREAT COMPROMISE AND
THE CONSIDERED DENIAL

These two motions are the most credible. Both result from honest and careful consideration of all points of view, as publicly expressed by the decisionmakers

In the great compromise, the motion maker tries to incorporate stipulations that meet all objections and that can be reasonably supported by as many other decisionmakers as possible. The motion maker often accepts stipulations and suggestions from the public and from the other decisionmakers in an attempt to satisfy as many concerns as possible. Though imperfect, the compromise treats all parties fairly. They are listened to.

When the great compromise is in the offing, make sure that the icing is on the cake. It will only be complete if you have developed your opposition agenda and have well established goals. It is not unusual for opponents to appear at public hearings believing that compromise is impossible, because of a seemingly intractable proponent or decisionmaking body. In this case, opponents are caught off guard, and when a compromise becomes possible, they don't know what to ask for. The decision adopted is incomplete.

The motion for considered denial uses the same considered approach with a different result. Decisionmakers fully discuss the pros and cons of the proposal and have an honest debate. Then the development proposal is turned down because no matter how many conditions are added to a possible approval, there are no conditions that could make it acceptable. In the considered denial, the decisionmakers believe that a level playing field is important and that a proponent should be treated with respect.

Considered denial is the preferred result for the opposition. To reach it, opponents must almost always present viable alternatives to the proposed development. And to maintain it, opponents must treat the decision and the proponent with the same respect and consideration that is shown by the decisionmakers.

Summary of Meeting Rules

Respect decorum.

Show empathy.

Avoid labels.

Stay fit.

Dress your part.

Understand the decisionmakers.

Count noses.

Be strategic in presenting the opposition's position.

Manage the clock.

Drive decisions.

IT ISN'T OVER UNTIL IT'S OVER

When opponents leave a public hearing with a decision denying the development proposal, it may mark the beginning, not the end, of the opposition effort. Land use challenge is usually a process, not an event. There is rarely a decision that is truly final. Zoning and planning decisions based on local ordinance, or agency decisions based on state or federal statute, tend to be temporary. Land use laws allocate rights and benefits among communities, neighborhoods, and development interests, and decisions tend to allocate development rights and benefits according to the values of today, not tomorrow. Proponents rarely go away. Land use proposals intended to use land or resources for their "highest and best economic use" or to meet a perceived public need often do so at the expense of the individual needs of neighbors and communities, or of scarce natural resources. Until the highest and best economic use or the public need is defined, the proponent will have more lives than the battery-driven bunny that has graced American TV for the last several years. Often there is no definitive resolution. Values change. Laws change. Politicians change. Decisionmakers change. What is unacceptable today may well be deemed acceptable tomorrow. Which leads to a post-meeting rule: *Be vigilant.* After public hearings are held and decisions rendered, do not let your guard down. Decisionmakers may feel remorse, and proponents aren't above making a motion for reconsideration. Many development plans are either not economically viable or can't be financed. In that case, the proponent will try to zone her way out of economic loss with greater intensity and additional uses. Or the same proposal may resurface in a slightly different package, one that incorporates some of the opposition's ideas.

In the case of the proposed South Lawrence Traffic Way in Lawrence, Kansas, or the proposed Montano Bridge across the Rio Grande in New Mexico, or the closure of the Fresh Kills landfill on Staten Island, the issue isn't going away even though a battle has been won. It won't go away until there is a resolution of how to move people on expressways around Lawrence, or how to move people more efficiently from Albuquerque across the Rio Grande to their homes and back again, or how to accommodate the need for solid waste disposal in New York City. Decisions have been made regarding the proposals, both for and against. But the problems that drive them remain.

Opposition leaders should view participation as an investment—of time, money, and emotional and intellectual energy. And after the heady rush of success in a public hearing, the opposition should act quickly to protect the value of the investment. The forces driving the development proposal will persevere. Will your opposition? Vigilance means protecting your investment. And protection begins at the ostensibly decisive public hearing. Here are several steps to help prevent a brutal land use battle from breaking out again:

1. Be a gracious winner and never a poor loser.

Given the high stakes of land use battles and the natural propensity to paint the participants in black and white, opposition members often act with knee-jerk emotionalism. They're wrong to do so. Most likely, the same proponent or members of his team will be part of your future. And they may well be part of an ultimate solution, such as finding an alternative to the development choice or scaling back a development proposal into a more acceptable form. Some day they may even be part of your team.

So don't burn your bridges. Regardless of the outcome, treat the decision, the decisionmakers, and the proponent with respect.

2. Look for alternatives.

Accept the fact that the development proposal is capable of resurrection. But remember, you will be stronger for the effort you make to prevent a replay of a protracted battle. If you are in a struggle with a neighbor, try to massage the wounds. If you are a neighborhood or community, approach the proponent agency or developer and negotiate land uses that reflect current community values.

In Vanderbilt Beach, Florida, Collier County attempted to locate a county boat ramp next to a residential neighborhood on property that was donated to the county for a park. The county staff could not find an alternative. The homeowner's association did: an undeveloped parcel that gave safer and more direct access to the Gulf of Mexico at a reasonable cost. The new site is wildly popular and the residential neighborhood has maintained the status quo.

3. Amend ordinances or change laws.

If the development proposal was incompatible but allowed by an ordinance or growth management plan, you can use your muscle to have the law changed. Otherwise, you are only one petition away from the next noncontextual proposal. Throughout the United States, current laws and ordinances are generally lax about land use compatibility. As a society we tend not to change the status quo until the last minute, when a planning crisis flares up. Burn your fuel on planning and ordinances that reflect the

CITIZENS CAN CHANGE LAWS

Citizens can change laws in a variety of ways. Many local governments formalize the process through a right of petition or referendum. However, even if a formal citizen process does not exist, most local governments rely on citizens' initiatives brought to their planning boards and councils through public petition.

community's vision, rather than letting the next development proposal define that vision for you.

4. Keep the opposition team together.

That a group tackled the challenge of opposition once does not mean that it will do so again. Stay in touch with those who were involved. They are the history. Their knowledge will become important when the existing board of decisionmakers and their staff have moved on and the next proponent tries to re-invent the history of the first proposal—the reasons for denial or approval, or the meaning of limiting conditions.

5. Preserve the record.

Keep copies of newspaper articles, minutes and attorney files, videotapes of public meetings, hearing transcripts, and the record of the decision, including all resolutions. When the next incompatible development proposal surfaces you will at least be prepared to educate new reporters, staff, and decisionmakers about what happened in the past.

6. Develop new leadership.

Make sure that a new generation of leadership understands the history of your area and is capable of fighting. Your experience is valuable in developing strong neighborhoods and communities.

7. Advocate strategies for long-term solutions.

Opponents should push for solutions that allocate rights and benefits permanently. If the allocation of rights and benefits is between neighbors, then site planning ought to be required that maximizes the rights between them. It isn't useful for one neighbor to achieve advantage over another.

If the allocation of rights and benefits is between a government proponent and private citizens, then the rights of private citizens should be weighed against the benefit of capital facility improvement or public resources enjoyed by the public as advanced by the government. As a community, ask whether there might be alternatives to the development choice that would minimize negative effects borne by communities and private citizens. Once again, citizens should push for municipal land uses which are the products of planning and vision.

If the allocation of rights and benefits is between a proponent developer and the public at large, then make a public choice. If, for instance, a developer wants to develop natural areas such as beaches, mountains, and wetlands, you might consider making those areas part of the public domain through acquisition. If the benefits are publicly shared, the lands should be public.

If, as opponents, you are able to allocate rights and benefits in a way that achieves real resolution, then your struggle will be over.

Be vigilant, because it isn't over until it's over.

CHAPTER 18

Litigation

*T*O litigate or not to litigate? That is the question that bedevils many an opponent who has failed to persuade the decisionmakers. My brief answer to this often complicated question is that in the great majority of cases, it is best not to litigate. The costs of litigation tend to outweigh its benefits.

However, there are times when litigation is the only remedy, usually when opponents aren't given the opportunity for a fair fight.

ENOUGH IS ENOUGH

Principle and passion—they are part of all protracted litigation and of virtually every land use struggle. Land use litigation is a lawyer's dream. Opponents tend to be passionate, and ready to fight, whatever the cost. To them a land use application may defy rational thought. The confrontation is one of principle. How could a proponent act so violently, so intrusively, destroying the fabric of a neighborhood, the viability of a business community, the serenity of the natural environment? How could the decisionmakers have been blind to the obvious merits of preservation and planning? Opponents feel as if a thief has been given the key to their home.

Before phoning the lawyer and initiating the process of redress, opponents should step back for some studied reflection, balancing their principle and passion with patience and reason. Litigation is a horrible process. It takes time. It is costly. It is unpredictable, often arbitrary. Judges and juries, often less familiar with the technical issues than the decisionmakers, are prone to reach even more illogical results. It is not unusual for litigants, fed up with the process, to settle part way through it for results that could have been achieved without any litigation at all.

The economic question whether to litigate at all ought to be considered first. What are the likely costs? What are the likely benefits? And what is the expected outcome? Using a statistician's approach, one would assign a value to the benefit, multiply it by the likelihood of success, and having obtained an expected value, would compare it to the cost. The greater number determines the decision. Higher cost, you don't litigate. Higher expected benefit, you do.

The trouble is that few lawyers can predict results confidently. And few can predict what a given result will ultimately mean. More litigation? Appeals? Or a return bout with the decisionmakers?

The road traveled by the Scenic Parkway Coalition of Charleston, South Carolina, is instructive. As reported by the local *Post and Courier,* the coalition took a developer all the way to the South Carolina Supreme Court for proposing that forty-seven live oaks be removed from a shopping center site.

First the developer was denied a construction permit by staff. On review, the local Board of Adjustments granted the permit over the staff's objection. Subsequently, the local circuit court upheld the Board of Adjustments, and the South Carolina Court of Appeals overturned the ruling of the Circuit Court. All of this culminated in the Supreme Court's reversal of the court of appeals decision, thus allowing removal of the trees approximately four years after the initial application.

The case illustrates two critical points. First, courts will almost always defer to the decisionmakers, which is what they are often bound to do by law. Judges do not make law; they interpret it and scrutinize procedure. As long as there is "clear and convincing" or "substantial competent" evidence in the record of local proceedings, judges will tend to support the decisionmakers. U.S. legal tradition presumes that local councils and boards best represent community values, and that they, along with state and federal agencies, have knowledge superior to that of courts on the issues they handle.

Second, the underlying objections to a development proposal may not be on firm legal ground. The clash between community values and local development laws is behind almost all land use disputes. Properties are zoned for development that is incompatible with surroundings. But what if communities have not planned for the preservation of open space, limited scale, or habitat preservation? In that case, opponents must grasp for whatever legal hooks there are. Did the members of the Scenic Coalition in Charleston believe that the proposed shopping center was inappropriate for the site, given its wooded character? Or was the real problem that zoning allowed noncontextual development in the first instance?

USE RESTRICTIONS

Restrictions on use might be private, as in the form of deed restrictions placed on property by prior owners; or they might be public, in the form of federal, state, or local laws or rules. Courts are loath to interfere in cases where restrictions are weak or nonexistent. Courts generally will not substitute their judgment for that of the original developer regarding the wisdom of including deed restrictions in original dedication documents, or of governmental bodies as related to the wisdom of adopting or interpreting zoning laws. So when citizens purchase property they should understand what deed restrictions, zoning, and federal and state laws both allow and prohibit.

In a neighbor versus neighbor battle, courts often ask why there wasn't some form of restriction adopted by the subdivision developer or local municipality that would have anticipated the land use conflict generated by the neighbor's proposal. A restriction could have prevented or avoided the proposal in the first instance. But the law often presumes that the neighbor affected by the proposal had notice—that it was his responsibility to anticipate every conceivable noncontextual development proposal that in theory might be allowed. The absence of formal restrictions can mean that an opponent has to challenge development by resorting to laws directed towards ancillary questions. For example, will a neighborhood be spared impacts associated with dumps and radioactive waste storage under nuisance theories? Can a river be spared by using common law theories of water rights?

There are few federal and state laws that protect whole ecosystems, and most of these apply to federally and state-owned land. This is a legal and cultural problem that may or may not be resolved some day. Meanwhile, should you, on your own, tackle the problem with limited resources?

Given the cost, uncertainty of outcome, tradition of deference to decisionmakers, and inadequacy of remedy in many cases, litigation should be a last alternative. Financial resources otherwise expended in litigation might better be used to change the system that produces incompatible land use, for instance by improving laws or running for political office. However, in special cases litigation may be the only remedy.

A FAIR FIGHT

A fair fight. Americans believe in the opportunity for a fair fight. Unfortunately, development proponents often don't fight fair. And public decisionmaking isn't always designed to encourage fair fights.

I describe a fair fight in its broadest sense, procedural fairness and intellectual honesty. The proponent's objective is to push a proposal from "guess" to yes as quickly as possible. For the proponent, time is money. Taking time to make considered decisions is therefore directly contrary to her interest. If she commits procedural irregularities or takes intellectual shortcuts to beat the clock, she exposes herself to litigation. Opponents who aren't allowed to fight fair before decisionmakers may well find a higher authority who gives them the right.

Proponents often fall into procedural traps, especially when they are confident that decisionmakers will vote in their favor.

Decisionmakers see no real need to go through the formalities of public presentation. They abbreviate meetings. They limit public discussion to the point where public input cannot be meaningful. They send a message to opponents that a proposed development will be built regardless of what objections might be raised.

Proponent municipalities are often the worst offenders because they play the dual role of advocating and approving the development choice. Governments are judge and jury. They design landfills, they approve landfills. They locate roads, they approve construction of roads. Proponent municipalities predetermine the outcome.

Generally, proponents also are better financed and have superior professional help to overwhelm opponents. Development proposals often represent choices in planning and science, and proponents will find and pay for professional advocates who support their proposals. Can opponents find and pay for professional advocates willing to expose the other side of the coin? If not, decisionmakers effectively see only one side.

Of course, what is often portrayed by the proponents' experts as fact is only opinion. It is not their role to expose multiple alternatives which, though more expensive, might work equally well. Without the accountability of competing views, other alternatives are never on the table for consideration.

Furthermore, many municipalities and state and federal agencies are ill equipped to properly evaluate expert opinions. How many municipalities have coastal geologists, hydrologists, and biologists on staff? They are outgunned by the proponent's staff.

Local opposition groups have the same disadvantage for different reasons. First, they usually have limited funding for experts and therefore rely on staff provided by the city, county, township, or state or federal agency. Second, they may not know how to find the appropriate expert, and find her quickly, especially in highly specialized disciplines. The proponent prepares his experts for months, while opponents prepare theirs in days, if at all.

Thus decisionmakers often make judgments without the benefit of fully developed arguments. When there is a one-dimensional view of multi-sided choices, a decision cannot be made with full intellectual honesty.

Upon review, judges may have limited discretion regarding substance. But judges understand the meaning of fairness. And if they see that a procedure was not fair, or that it was not approached with intellectual honesty, they may tell the decisionmakers to start over and do it again. Litigation is the brickbat that gets the decisionmakers' attention the second time around.

There are two final points that opponents should consider. The first is that the cases with the highest probability of success are those where the opponents prepared a record from the beginning and contacted a lawyer early on. If an attorney is approached only after public hearings have been held, it will be far more difficult for her to advise opponents to litigate.

The second point is that "a good case" shouldn't automatically translate into a decision to litigate. There should be a relationship between the task and the ability of opposition. A strong environmental organization with litigation experience is probably better equipped than a small underfunded citizen's group to save a habitat or a natural resource. But if the opponent's goal is to prevent his neighbor from destroying his property value and quality of life, then he is the one best equipped for the fight. If the choice affects a community, litigation may be a one-shot effort for the civic association that cannot be missed.

There are times when principle and passion, patience and reason, all dictate that as opponents you will receive the benefit of a fight that is procedurally fair and intellectually honest. Litigation may be the only remedy.

Is enough enough, or is litigation your only remedy?

CONCLUSION

Gaining Perspective

Opposition that becomes an end in itself is as devoid of spirit and thought as the incompatible proposal that initiated it in the first place. When this happens it is time to call a halt; to step back and view what has happened in terms not of simple results, but rather of life's experience.

Much good comes out of the experience of opposition—win, lose, or draw. New friends. A new understanding of science, planning or decisionmaking. Public awareness. Pride in community. Whether you win or lose or end up somewhere in between, something good is always achieved. You have done what few people do: you have contributed to your community, your neighborhood, and your country in a meaningful way, by fostering public debate which inevitably improves the quality of land use choices which your community makes. You have participated in the democratic process.

Perhaps your fortitude and unselfish dedication to a good cause will also serve you well in future life endeavors. No doubt you have a richer grasp of local politics and its procedures, which can be shared with others who are confronted with similar problems. Certainly you are wiser about people and the way they interact.

Wiser too, perhaps, about yourself and your limits. Wise enough to know when to let go of the past and move on to other things. You and the people who depend on you will be the better for it.

Man is a relatively recent steward of the earth who has had an incommensurably large impact on it, changing the composition of its air and its water and its land. Developers are fond of pointing out that man will always change his surroundings. Why try to maintain the status quo? Why preserve? Why resist change, when resistance goes against man's nature?

Change is not the issue. The *type* of change is. If man should be so fortunate as to survive another thousand years or 100,000 years, how will future generations judge our present one? Cars will probably be viewed as a crude mode of transportation. Pollution of water to accommodate manufacturing, barbaric. Destruction of the rain forests, plain stupid. Will future generations act more responsibly than we have?

We are responsible for the choices we make. If we design our home at the expense of our neighbor, that is a choice. If we use landfills instead of recycling, that is a choice. If we harden our beaches with concrete or desecrate our forests and destroy their value as habitat for other species calling earth home, that is a choice. Our choices reflect our view of responsibility, as individuals, as communities, and as a society.

If we view ourselves in the vacuum of the here and now, then we are likely to take a very narrow view of our responsibility. If we view ourselves as stewards of our communities, country, and planet, then our notion of responsibility is likely to be more generous: Our influence is long lasting.

If, in some courtroom in the sky, generations past were to try to defend their development choices to us, they could plead ignorance. There was much they just did not know as a matter of scientific or quantitative fact. Our generation does not have the same excuse. We know a lot, and more each day. With satellites, geographic information systems, the Internet, and all the other available technology, we might plead information overload, but not its lack.

And technological advances are speeding up. Soon we won't be limited to decisions made from blue line drawings tacked to bulletin boards, or voluminous reports tucked away in staff files for private consideration. Municipal, state, and federal governments will require that development plans and expert reports be posted on the Internet for public scrutiny and comment. Remote experts will testify electronically, rebutting each other and thereby advancing the boundaries of local wisdom. Viewing images in 3D on the Internet, citizens will be able to visualize proposed roads, stadiums, parks, and other public facilities in relation to their surroundings. Before they are built, all alternatives will be examined. Incompatible development won't be foisted on the politically weak so easily. There will be more public accountability on the part of decisionmakers and public officials. Videotaped deliberations will be a required part of the public record, available for instant recall to anyone with tomorrow's cross between a television and computer.

But today is not tomorrow. It is the bridge to tomorrow. Each neighborhood has its own vision of how to build that bridge. There is no one set of values that is right for every community. Farmland preservation might be prized in one area and put low on the list of priorities in a neighboring area. The question isn't what the particular value is, but rather what priority is given to various values.

The proponent asks: What will maximize the value of the property? What will facilitate construction of my public project? Is the proposal politically achievable? These are postage-stamp-world questions. Before they are asked, the community should examine other questions: What would the possible effects be of certain types of development on the community and on the environment? What choices would maximize public and private benefit? How does one parcel of land relate to another, and how does development affect the long-term viability of ecological systems?

Your public participation places the questions in the right order. If you've read this far, you are the kind of person who values integrated development, not postage stamp solutions.

You should never apologize for confronting poor development before it happens. There is no shame in wanting a better living environment for our families, more functional communities for our citizens, or laws to preserve our natural resources. It is okay to press governments to be intelligent in their land planning. Our involvement pressures local, state, and federal governments to make better choices. In some small way, it fulfills our responsibility to strive for a better tomorrow.

In our ongoing challenge to achieve reasoned development, there is no one magical formula for success. But I hope I have provided some insight that will help you in your particular challenge. If you elect to pursue that challenge, do so wisely. Think and act strategically. And in the end, may your challenge be thoughtful, your efforts fulfilling, and may your community have the good fortune to make choices that withstand the test of time.

Organizational Resource List

Below is a list of national organizations involved in planning, environmental, and civic issues. These are my suggestions for frequently used resources that may be of use to the reader. The provision of this list is simply for the convenience of the reader. These organizations have not endorsed any of the opinions expressed in this book, which opinions are strictly my own.

"None of the organizations listed below has in any way endorsed the materials or opinions in this book, which opinions are strictly my own, nor are any of these organizations affiliated with the author or the book in any way."

Alliance for Redesigning Government
1120 G Street NW, Suite 850
Washington, D.C. 20005
www.alliance.napawash.org/alliance/index.html

American Coastal Coalition
1667 K Street NW, Suite 480
Washington, D.C. 20006
www.coastalcoalition.org

American Farm Land Trust
1920 M Street NW, Suite 400
Washington, D.C. 20035
www.farmland.org

American Institute of Architects
National Headquarters
1735 New York Ave. NW
Washington, D.C. 20005

American Institute of City Planners
M-NCPPC
801 Pennsylvania Ave. NW #1113
Washington, D.C. 20004
www.planning.org/index.html

American Planning Association
122 S. Michigan Ave., Suite 1600
Chicago, IL 60603
www.planning.org/index.html

American Public Transit Association
1201 New York Ave. NW
Washington, D.C. 20005

American Rivers
1025 Vermont Ave. NW
Suite 720
Washington, D.C. 20005
www.amrivers.org

American Shore and Beach Preservation Association
Business Office
1724 Indian Way
Oakland, CA 94611
www2.ncsu.edu/ncsu/CIL/ncsu_kenan/shore_beach/index.html

American Society of Highway and Transportation Officials
444 W. Capital Street NW, Suite 249
Washington, D.C. 20001
www.aashto.org

American Society of Landscape Architects
636 Eye Street NW
Washington, D.C. 20001-3736
www.asla.org

Biodiversity Conservation Network
Biodiversity Support Program
C/O World Wildlife Fund
1250 24th Street NW
Washington, D.C. 20037
http://bcnet.org

**Center for Excellence in Sustainable Development,
Resource Data Base**
U.S. Department of Energy
Office of Energy Efficiency and Renewable Energy
Denver Regional Support Office
1617 Cole Blvd.
Golden, CO 80401
www.ncat.org.7050/

Center for Understanding the Built Environment
5328 W 67th Street
Praire Village, KS 66208
www.cubekc.org

Civic.com
www.fcw-civic.com

**Context Institute's Sustainable Culture
Information Services**
www.context.org

Cyburbia.org
www.cyburbia.org

Envirolink
The Envirolink Network
4618 Hincy Street
Pittsburgh, PA 15213
www.envirolink.org

Environmental Protection Agency's Transportation Partners Project
Environmental Protection Agency
401 M Street SW
Washington, D.C. 20460
www.epa.gov/tp/

Forest World
The Forest Partnership Inc.
PO Box 426
161 Austin Drive #7
Burlington, VT 05402
www.forestworld.com

Friends of the Earth
1025 Vermont Ave. NW
Suite 300
Washington, D.C. 20005-6303
www.foe.org

International Environmental Information Network
4801 W. 81st Street
Minneapolis, MN 55437
www.envirobiz.com

International Healthy Cities Foundation
2001 Addison Street
Berkeley, CA 90704-1102

International Historic Society
www.monumental.com/lhf/

Joint Center for Sustainable Communities
National Association of Counties
440 1st Street NW, Suite 800
Washington D.C. 20001
www.naco.org/programs/special/center/index.cfm

Lincoln Institute of Land Policy
113 Brattle Street
Cambridge, MA 02138-3400
www.lincolnist.edu/main.html

Lighthouse Preservation Society
4 Middle Street
Newburyport, MA 01950
www.maine.com/lights.lps.htm

Mountain Institute
Main & Dogwood Streets
PO Box 907
Franklin, WV 26807
www.mountain.org

National Academy of Sciences
2101 Constitution Ave. NW
Washington, D.C. 20418
www.nas.edu

National Association of Counties
440 1st Street NW
Eighth Floor
Washington, D.C. 20001
www.naco.org

National Association of Development Organizations
444 N. Capital Street, Suite 630
Washington, D.C. 20001

National Association of Towns and Townships
and
National Association for Small Communities
444 N. Capital Street SW
Suite 208
Washington, D.C. 20001-1202

National Center for Appropriate Technology
3040 Continental Drive
Butte, Montana 59702
www.ncat.org

National City Government Resource Center
National Civic League
1445 Market Street, Suite 300
Denver, CO 80202-1728

National Government Home Page
http://localgov.org

National Institute for the Environment
1725 K Street NW, Suite 212
Washington, D.C. 20006-1401
www.cnie.org

National League of Cities
1301 Pennsylvania Ave. NW
Washington, D.C. 20004-1763

National Library for the Environment
1725 K Street NW, Suite 212
Washington, D.C. 20006-1401
www.cnie.org/nle/

Nature Conservancy
International Headquarters
1815 North Lynn Street
Arlington, VA 22209

National Resources Defense Council
40 West 20th Street
New York, NY 10011
www.nrdc.org/worldview/index.html

National Trust for Historical Preservation
1785 Massachusetts Ave. NW
Washington, D.C. 20036
www.nthp.org

Partnership for a Walkable America
National Safety Council
1121 Spring Lake Drive
Itasca, IL 60143-3201
www.tfhrc.gov/safety/pedsbike/pedwlk.htm

Planners Web – Planning Commissioner's Journal
www.plannersweb.com

Rocky Mountain Institute Green Development Services
1739 Snowmass Creek Road
Snowmass, CO 81654-9199
www.rmi.org/gds/whatis.htm

Scenic America
21 Dupont Circle
Washington, D.C. 20036
www.transact.org/sa/scenic/htm

Sierra Club
85 2nd Street, 2nd Floor
San Francisco, CA 94105-3441
www.sierraclub.org

Turner-Fairbank Highway Research Center
www.tfhrc.gov

The Urban Land Institute
1025 Thomas Jefferson Street NW
Suite 500 W
Washington, D.C. 20007-5201
www.uli.org

U.S. Environmental Protection Agency
401 M Street SW
Washington, D.C. 20460
www.epa.gov

U.S. Green Building Council
90 New Montgomery Street
Suite 1001
San Francisco, CA 94105

USGS San Francisco/Bay Area
http:.//sfbay.wr.usgs.gov/access/access_sfb.html

Wildlife Conservation Society
www.wcs.org

World Forest Institute
4033 SW Canyon Road
Portland, OR 97221
www.vpm.com/wfi/

World Resources Institute
1709 New York Ave. NW
Washington, D.C. 20006
www.wri.org

World Wildlife Fund
1250 24th Street NW
PO Box 96555
Washington, D.C. 20077-7795
www.wwfus.org

Independent Reviews

"Just read "There Goes the Neighborhood" over the weekend and am really taken with it. It seems obvious that someone should have written a book like it a long time ago but I've never seen such a useful treatment of what is usually a supersensitive subject. I was a member of Santa Fe's Community Development Commission years ago, was a founder of the Santa Fe Canyon Association and founder of the Santa Fe Federation of Neighborhood Associations and a book like yours would have been immensely useful over the years. It's a great guide for practical action and a helpful road map."

David J. Padwa Santa Fe, New Mexico

"PageSoutherlandPage is currently doing comprehensive community planning for the city of Cedar Park, just northwest of Austin, Texas. The community has grown from a population of 5,500 in 1990 to over 18,000 in 1998, with continued growth to 40-50,000 expected in the next 15 years. I am part of a team of urban planners, land planners, architects, engineers, transportation consultants, and economic development specialists working to help Cedar Park plan for its future. I personally led a week's worth of back-to-back meetings and community forums to help the community clarify its vision for itself. So with those experiences freshly in mind, I found your book timely and worthwhile. In particular, I valued your perspective on the wide range of issues in community planning."

Kurt M. Neubek, AIA , Director of Strategic Services, PageSoutherlandPage, Houston, Texas.

"I just had to write and tell you what a great job you have done. It is GREAT and so much needed. Everything you say is right on and represents exactly what happens."... "The content is excellent, complete, and easy to understand."

Dr. Faye Biles, former chancellor Kent State University, President of Marco Island Civic Association, Marco Island, Florida

"I enjoyed getting the chance to read this and offer comments. The memories flooded back to me time after time as I read this. I can recall time and again situations that could have been changed if either side would have read this in advance and done something different. The names and cases changed but the mistakes are too often repeated and perpetuated."

Paul Muenzer, former mayor of Akron, Ohio and Naples,Florida.; former chairman of the Southwest Florida Regional Planning Council.

"This is a very well written, coherent land use case/planning guide for anybody who lives anywhere. All of us are impacted by the forces described by Kim Kobza, and the statement on page [ ] says it all "The lack of congruence between community values and local development laws underlies almost all land disputes."

I served on a county planning board for 11 years. We are a half rural, half urban area with a major university of 20,000 and historical areas dating back to 1710 or so. Every problem mentioned by the author was experienced by the board at one time or another. I wish this book had been available to us. It would have been of tremendous help in a time of rapid growth and environmental stress, and I plan to recommend it to everybody I know involved in public policy and planning. At last we are not alone."

Sharlene G. Pilkey,
Raleigh, North Carolina,

"There Goes the Neighborhood is a book that never strays from the important topic it addresses. It is amazingly practical in the sense that it's a manual. It's well written and has lovely metaphors and analogs. It is chock full of useful wisdom. From citizen activist from developer to banker, There Goes the Neighborhood should be at the ready. A treasure."

John O'Neil, President of Center for Leadership Renewal, Author of Paradox of Success and Leadership Aikido, San Francisco, California.

"As someone who has been on every "side" of land use cases in positions ranging from local community group volunteer to city official, I found "There Goes the Neighborhood" a very useful how to guide to land use and development issues. The book includes important lessons learned for individuals just getting involved in the field as well as for sophisticated developers. The style is both easy to read and entertaining, a difficult accomplishment for this subject matter."

Emily Menlo Marks, Executive Director, United Neighborhood Houses of New York and former Administrator of the New York City Environmental Protection Agency. New York City, New York.